CRIME FREE

MICHAEL CASTLEMAN

SIMON AND SCHUSTER

New York

Copyright © 1984 by Michael Castleman
All rights reserved
including the right of reproduction
in whole or in part in any form
Published by Simon and Schuster
A Division of Simon & Schuster, Inc.
Simon & Schuster Building
Rockefeller Center
1230 Avenue of the Americas
New York, New York 10020
SIMON AND SCHUSTER and colophon are
registered trademarks of Simon & Schuster, Inc.
Designed by Christopher Simon
Manufactured in the United States of America

10 9 8 7 6 5 4 3 2

LIBRARY OF CONGRESS CATALOGING IN PUBLICATION DATA
Castleman, Michael.
   Crime free.

   Bibliography: p.
   Includes index.
   1. Crime prevention—Citizen participation.   2. Crime
prevention—United States—Citizen participation.
I. Title.
HV7431.C37   1984   364.4′0458   84-1273
ISBN 0-671-45172-3

Grateful acknowledgment is made to Harper & Row, Publishers, Inc., for permission
to reprint material from *The Battered Woman*, copyright © 1979 by Lenore E.
Walker.

To Mildred and Louis Castleman

Acknowledgments

Deepest thanks to David Castleman.

Special thanks to John Brockman, Daniel and Steven Castleman, Kate Connell, Steve Faigenbaum, David Fenton, Fred Hills, Jonathan King, Katinka Matson, Paul Rupert, Anne Simons, and Wendy Zheutlin.

And many thanks to the American Association of Retired Persons, Frank Browning, Violet Chu, Dennis Church, Community Boards Program, Tom Cox, Crary/St. Mary's Community Council, Peter Crosby, Delancey Street Foundation, Detroit Police Chief William Hart, Detroit Police Crime Prevention Section, Dimond Community Safety Patrol, Terry Dobson, Emerge, Judith Fein, Tom Ferguson, Henry Giaretto, Betty Grayson, James Humphrey, Kathy Hoard, Inmate Project, Ray Johnson, Kew Gardens Civilian Patrol, Joel Kirsch, Norbert Kozlowski, George Leonard, Hazel Manica, *Medical Self-Care Magazine,* Men Overcoming Violence (MOVE), Patrick Murphy, National Association of Town Watch, National Center for Community Crime Prevention, National Committee for the Prevention of Child Abuse, National Council on Crime and Delinquency, National Criminal Justice Reference Service, National Organization for Victim Assistance (NOVA), National Retired Teachers Association, Pacific News Service, Parents United, Matthew Peskin, Rick Pirman, Carole Pisarczyk, Police Foundation, San Francisco Police Crime Prevention Unit, Santa Clara County Comprehensive Child Sexual Abuse Treatment Program, Nelson Scheuer, Amitai Schwartz, Security Training Institute, Leonard Sipes, Raymond Shonholtz, Eddie Solis, Daniel Sonkin, Harrison A. "Skip" Stubbs, Southland Corporation, George Sunderland, Tenderloin Senior Escort Program, Joseph Trommer, Frank Viviano, Jan Williams, Ellie Wegener, Women Organized to Make Abuse Nonexistent (W.O.M.A.N.) Inc., and James Wright.

Contents

ALSO BY MICHAEL CASTLEMAN

Sexual Solutions

Anyone Can Become Much Safer

This book is intended for anyone who would like to become safer from crime and violence. To do so, you need not become a black belt in the martial arts, live in an electronic fortress, keep a handgun by your bed or tear gas on your keychain. You don't need to spend a great deal of money. You don't even have to be able-bodied. Despite what the mass media and many law enforcement officials say about crime "raging out of control," regardless of your age, sex, race, occupation, income, neighborhood, physical limitations, or past crime experiences, you can substantially reduce your risk of criminal victimization.

This promise rests on solid evidence. Individuals who incorporate easy-to-learn techniques into their lives can reduce their risk of assault, robbery, and rape by up to 90 percent. Communities that implement simple, low-cost, neighborhood crime-prevention programs can cut their crime rates up to 88 percent. The concepts and techniques that make these rapid crime-rate reductions possible are the central focus of this book.

"THE BUSINESS OF EVERY AMERICAN"

The case for personal and neighborhood crime prevention is so compelling, so solidly rooted in common sense and traditional American self-reliance, that it could revolutionize the way we deal with crime. It's tragic—"criminal" if you will—that in our collective horror at the crime problem, we have lost faith in our ability to take care of ourselves and each other. Instead, we have relegated the problem to the police, the courts, and the social welfare agencies. The public should certainly support good work in these areas, but the crime problem is simply too important to be left just to them.

In its 1967 report, the President's Crime Commission wrote: "Combatting crime is the business of every American." None of us can afford to abdicate our personal responsibility. The criminal justice system cannot guarantee our well-being anymore than physicians can guarantee our health. Each of us must take primary responsibility for our own health, with doctors as back-up consultants called upon, one would hope, as little as possible. Similarly, each of us must take primary responsibility for our own safety, with the police called upon as little as possible. This is not a utopian vision. It's an everyday reality for a growing number of individuals, businesses, and communities around the United States.

There's no mystery to effective crime prevention. It's mostly common sense. It's also empowering, fulfilling, and enjoyable. Those who practice it reduce their victimization risk quickly and substantially and gain greater control over their lives.

A PERSONAL QUEST

I am not a police officer, criminologist, black belt, or locksmith. I'm a journalist who specializes in self-help writing, whose background is in community organizing. My interest in the crime problem dates back to the night in 1974 when I was mugged at gunpoint. That experience, and the burglary of my home the following year, launched me on a personal quest to discover the elements of effective crime-prevention.

My search led me to organize The Inmate Project, which placed three hundred tutors in ten Michigan jails and prisons. It led to three years of karate training. It also took me around the country to examine firsthand some of the programs that have dramatically reduced many communities' crime rates. I participated in community meetings, home security surveys, and street patrols with police and neighborhood residents. My quest led me to join my neighbors in organizing our apartment building in San Francisco for greater security. I also became active in the Community Boards Program in my neighborhood, an innovative organization that helps neighbors settle their disputes before they escalate to the point where the police must intervene. Finally, I became proficient in the use of tear gas and handguns.

From the start, I endeavored to suspend my prior beliefs and ask, "What *really* prevents crime?" I decided to accept no crime-prevention recommendations on faith, but rather to insist on documented evidence of effectiveness. This approach confirmed some of my previous beliefs: the pivotal role of community organizing, and the folly of believing that larger, more heavily armed police forces deter much crime. But it also produced some surprises. I changed my mind about several former convictions, notably the idea that poverty and unemployment are the chief causes of crime, and my once-strong belief in handgun registration. Finally, some ideas I'd never appreciated emerged as crucial to the crime problem: domestic violence and the demographics of the Baby-Boom generation.

It was a long haul. By the end, I became convinced that crime has less to do with "them"—the poor, the unemployed, the police, the courts, or the producers of violent TV shows—than it does with all of "us," and how we live our lives, whatever our circumstances.

BEYOND HOPELESSNESS AND CYNICISM

Ask people, "What really prevents crime?" and most reactions reflect despair. Many shake their heads and say, "Nothing works." These feelings are certainly understandable. Every day the media bombard us with what law enforcement and elected officials tout as "solutions" to the crime problem, and every day much of the rest of the news proves them wrong.

Some say we need more police, but in the last ten years that's exactly what we've gotten and the crime rate has not declined. Others say we need more prisons and stiffer sentences. Again, that's what we've gotten but the crime rate has not declined. Some say we need full employment and an end to discrimination. These are important, but rather remote, goals. If we accept this perspective, we must resign ourselves to a high crime rate for a long time, probably forever. No wonder so many people feel cynical about the crime problem.

But around the country, those involved in personal and neighborhood crime-prevention efforts feel uniformly optimistic, even ebullient, and with good reason. Their efforts have produced rapid, dramatic crime-rate reductions at low cost, *without* more police and more prisons and *without* full employment and an end to discrimination. In fact, some of the most successful crime-prevention programs have developed in communities so hurt by the economic reverses of recent years that they were forced to *lay off* many police.

How can our leaders seem so bereft of ideas, when so many grassroots efforts have produced such remarkable results? The answer comes into clearer focus if we consider crime as a disease.

THE EPIDEMIOLOGY OF CRIME

It may seem odd to frame the crime problem in terms of a disease epidemic, but that is how most authorities describe it, as a "plague," a "cancer" that has "infected" the body politic. It has "spread" everywhere, and no one is "immune." Crime is a "symptom" of a "sick society," and the "cure," some would argue, requires "strong medicine."

But crime has more than a metaphorical relationship to the public health. Homicide is now the leading cause of death for black men age fifteen to twenty-four and is ninth for men of all ages. Furthermore, fear of crime takes a terrible toll on the nation's mental health.

Epidemiologists divide "prevention" into three categories: primary, secondary, and tertiary. Primary prevention eliminates the breeding grounds of disease agents—draining swamps to eradicate the mosquitoes that transmit malaria. Secondary prevention enhances the host's ability to defend itself against disease—vaccinations against polio. Tertiary prevention attacks the disease agent after it has caused infection—antibiotics to kill bacteria.

In the epidemiology of crime, primary prevention is the cornerstone of the liberal approach, hence the calls to eliminate the so-called "breeding grounds" of crime: poverty, unemployment, discrimination, drug abuse, and inferior housing and education. Conservatives prefer tertiary prevention: more severe punishment for criminals. Social programs are certainly necessary; so are police, courts, and prisons. But our political leaders have consistently overemphasized primary and tertiary prevention, while underestimating host-resistance approaches. This is truly tragic, because *secondary-prevention programs produce the largest, fastest, most consistent and cost-effective reductions in the crime rate.*

THE QUIET REVOLUTION

The nation's leaders may not appreciate the effectiveness of secondary crime prevention, but at the grassroots level, millions of Americans have become much safer because of it. In the last ten years, a quiet revolution has gained momentum throughout the United States. People have become as disenchanted with the government/law enforcement/welfare approach to the crime problem as they have with crime itself. In classic American fashion, they have taken matters into their own hands—not as members of lynch mobs, but as responsible citizens who have every right to do what they can to bring peace, harmony, and safety to their communities.

Whenever nonprofessionals get involved in crime prevention, the charge of "vigilantism" rears its ugly head. In view of the more sordid chapters of American history, the dangers of mob rule must always be kept in mind, but given the urgency and magnitude of today's crime problem, the risk of vigilantism is quite small. Self-help crime-prevention efforts bear striking resemblance to emergency first aid. They are no closer to mob rule than first aid is to practicing medicine without a license.

These days, signs of the quiet revolution are everywhere. Classes in self-defense, rape prevention, tear gas and handgun training abound. Many communities have organized neighborhood watches, community patrols, senior escort services, mediation boards, victim assistance programs, and organizations to deal with incest, child abuse, and woman battering. And in the last decade, enlightened police departments have established crime-prevention units staffed by officers who work as community organizers to assist self-help efforts. Some forward-looking police departments have even begun to evolve away from traditional "reactive" policing toward what they call "proactive" work, in support of neighborhood crime-prevention groups.

Given the emotional intensity of the political crime debate, it's noteworthy that successful grassroots groups approach crime prevention from a nonpartisan perspective. This is not to say that the members are apolitical; if anything, crime prevention appeals to those with strong political beliefs. But politics seems curiously beside the point when you're trying to catch a neighborhood rapist or train senior citizens in assault avoidance. Political arguments are counterproductive because they alienate neighbors from each other, while effective crime prevention depends on united action. The programs that work best are based not on partisan politics, but on neighborliness and common sense. I feel privileged to have met so many crime-prevention activists in various parts of the United States. This book is both a tribute to, and a compendium of, their efforts.

HOW TO USE THIS BOOK

Chapters 1 and 2 are case studies that demonstrate the astonishing success crime-prevention programs can achieve, even under the most challenging circumstances. Chapter 3 provides background information on crime, criminals, and their victims. Chapters 4 through 8 discuss how to prevent violent and theft crimes, how to organize a neighborhood crime-prevention group, and how to support a loved one's recovery from criminal victimization. Chapter 9 examines the supremely important, but often neglected, area of domestic violence: woman battering, child abuse, and incest. Chapter 10 shows why neither the liberal nor conservative approaches to the crime problem have worked, and why self-help efforts have produced such remarkable results. Chapter 11 examines the subject of guns, their use and abuse, and shows why neither gun laws nor gun ownership has contributed significantly to crime prevention. Resources for readers can be found at the end of each chapter.

Most books on this subject imply that personal safety requires major lifestyle changes. A few minor adjustments might well be necessary; a dozen, perhaps; but major changes? No way. To feel safer, the central task is to place your personal and neighborhood crime problem in perspective, then to implement the suggestions that make the most sense to you.

I'm under no illusions about the possibility of becoming invulnerable to crime. There is always some irreduceable risk of being in the wrong place at the wrong time. But those who incorporate the suggestions in this book into their lives should quickly become much safer. If enough people implemented personal crime-prevention programs, we could reduce the nation's crime rate 50 percent in five years.

The crime issue needs to be demystified. It is neither as complicated nor as hopeless as the media and our political leaders have made it appear. We *can* cut the crime rate quickly and substantially without social upheaval and without spending a great deal of money. The suggestions in this book have documented effectiveness. They *work*. Millions of people have used them to become much safer. You can too.

1

How 7-Eleven Reduced
Armed Robberies by 56 Percent

At first glance, 7-Eleven stores would appear to be perfect targets for armed robberies. Open late at night when the majority of hold-ups occur, most are staffed by a single individual, often a woman. Many are located in high-crime areas, where poverty, unemployment, and drug abuse are serious problems. And despite the clear risks involved in working in such an exposed position, the company that owns the 7-Eleven chain, Southland Corporation of Dallas, Texas, forbids its employees to keep guns—or any weapons—in the stores.

According to the FBI, holdups at convenience stores have increased a staggering 47 percent since 1976. The average cash loss reached $607, and thousands of salespeople fell victim to aggravated assault (with a weapon). But during the same period, the 7,000 stores in the 7-Eleven chain had a decidedly different experience: robberies plummeted 56 percent; crime-related injuries declined 50 percent; and cash losses fell 66 percent to just $45.

How did 7-Eleven do it? With a low-cost crime-prevention program so simple and subtle, most customers don't even notice it. But robbers do.

HELP WANTED: EX-ARMED ROBBERS

The 7-Eleven program was developed in consultation with 56-year-old Ray Johnson, an expert in armed robbery. He should be. He spent twenty-five years in California prisons on robbery convictions. After his parole in 1968, Johnson learned that the Western Behavioral Sciences Institute (WBSI) in La Jolla, California, was interested in hiring some ex-armed robbers as consultants to an unusual crime-prevention project, whose goal was to redesign retail stores to make them less vulnerable to holdups. Johnson and several other former robbers pooled their experiences and developed a program that WBSI tested at 120 7-Elevens in Southern California in 1975. Sixty stores made the minor robbery-prevention alterations the ex-robbers recommended. The other sixty did not. After eight months, the unmodified stores showed no change in robbery victimization, but robberies at the modified 7-Elevens *dropped 30 percent.*

The experiment made a tremendous impression on Southland executives, most of whom had started as 7-Eleven sales clerks and knew firsthand the risks of working in convenience stores. They hired Johnson to work with the company's security division as a permanent crime-prevention consultant. Together, they refined the WBSI recommendations and in 1976 launched what has become the nation's most successful robbery-prevention program.

ELEGANT AND IMAGINATIVE

Here's how it works: Cash registers have been moved up front. Display advertising that once covered all windows has been moved to leave the registers visible from the street. Exterior floodlights have been installed. Both registers and sales clerks have been placed on raised platforms, and beneath each register, special timed-access safes have been installed. Finally, store properties have been redesigned to eliminate alley exits and to channel traffic to and from the streets out front. Minor changes, but they make a tremendous difference to robbers.

"The typical robber," Johnson says, "prefers concealment. He's looking for a store with the cash register not visible from the street." The robbery-prevention program makes 7-Eleven cash registers highly visible. By moving them up front, removing window advertising, and installing outside floodlights, the typical 7-Eleven cash register becomes "spotlighted," an effect that puts the would-be robber "on stage," which is the last place he wants to be. Increased visibility means increased risk of apprehension. As a result, the robber is more likely to think twice before attempting a holdup.

Most robbers consider their escape options before pulling their guns. By eliminating alley exits, 7-Eleven has eliminated robbers' preferred escape routes. Channeling traffic to and from the front of the store also increases the likelihood that the clerk will be able to tell police which way a robber flees.

Raising the cash register further frustrates the holdup man. "The typical robber," Johnson says, "wants to make sure there's enough money in the register to justify the risk of attempting the robbery. He makes a small purchase—candy or cigarettes—and as the clerk rings up the sale, he checks the cash drawer. If he sees bulging compartments of tens and twenties he pulls his gun." Placing the register on a raised platform above the robber's eye level prevents him from casing the cash drawer. Clerks also stand on raised platforms, which makes them look more imposing and provides a small but significant psychological advantage.

A major component of the robbery-prevention program is the safe, the Timed Access Cash Controller (TACC). Designed in consultation with Ray Johnson and manufactured by Southland subsidiary Tidel Systems, TACCs have an ingenious two-compartment design. They hold a great deal of money in one compartment, but dispense only a little at a time from the other. As tens and twenties accumulate, clerks deposit them in the TACC's storage compartment. Clerks do not have keys to their TACCs; they are emptied by store managers during the day, never at night when most robberies occur. If a transaction calls for more change than the register contains, the clerk presses a button and from its dispensing compartment, the TACC releases a plastic tube with $10 in small bills and change. The average purchase at 7-Eleven comes to $1.57, so $10 in change usually lasts several minutes. Each TACC disbursement, however, triggers a timer that prevents another disbursement for two minutes.

What's to stop robbers from forcing 7-Eleven clerks to keep pushing TACC release buttons every two minutes until all funds have been disbursed?

"It takes too much time," Johnson explains. "With the register so visible from the street, no robber would hold a gun on anyone that long. Most robberies take place in less than one minute. When you're worried about getting caught—and every robber is *very worried* every time—two minutes is an eternity. It's just not worth it to wait that long for another $10. You want to flash your gun, get the cash, and split." When TACCs are installed, large decals are affixed to the store's front doors: "Register contains less than $30. Timelock safe clerk cannot open."

What's to stop robbers from shooting, raping, or kidnapping clerks in frustration over such small takes?

"That just hasn't happened," Southland Security Manager Richard Nelson explains. "Our robbery-related casualties have gone way down since we launched the crime-prevention program. Our experience has been that robbers frustrated by small takes don't shoot; they leave. Recently in Wilmington, Delaware, a man asked for cigarettes, then pulled a pistol. But when he saw how little was in the register, he left with just the cigarettes. He didn't even take the money. In Philadelphia, we had a robber who got so disgusted with the $11 in the register, he threw it back in the clerk's face and left."

Johnson says, "You hear a lot these days about 'crazy criminals shooting people for no reason.' It happens, but most robbers don't shoot people to punish them for a small take. They shoot if the victim does something to rattle them, something either stupid or heroic. All robbers, except the very few who are truly insane, want to get the job done as quickly and smoothly as possible. They don't want to hurt anyone, but they're very tense and usually on drugs or alcohol. They're not crazy, but they're not rational either. You don't want to do anything to startle them. You don't want to give them the slightest excuse to hurt you."

That's why Southland trains its employees how to respond if confronted by a robber. The rule is: Keep it short and smooth. Clerks are instructed to obey robbers' orders, not to argue, and not to attempt any heroics by fighting or chasing after them. "That's how people get hurt," Johnson says.

Clerks are taught to greet each customer personally—with eye contact—a good business practice, and a signal to would-be robbers that they have been noticed and might be identified later. If anyone attempts a holdup, clerks are instructed to remain as calm as possible and to concentrate on the robber's description. They estimate the robber's height as he leaves, with the aid of conspicuous tape measures affixed to 7-Eleven front door frames. The tape measures are part of the "Robbery Prevention Kit" Tidel Systems markets in addition to the TACC safe.

"The tape measures are powerful robbery deterrents," Johnson says. "As the would-be robber approaches the store, he sees the lighting, the visible register, and the limited escape situation. He starts thinking, this doesn't feel right. Once inside, he sees the TACC decals and the tape measure on the door and he decides, this isn't worth it."

Clerks who get robbed are trained to notice which way the robber flees and to get a description and license number of any getaway car. Then they call the police. While waiting, the clerk fills out a "Robbery Profile Form," with the robber's description, flight direction, vehicle, and weapon used. Despite Southland's ban on weapons, clerks are taught to recognize the handguns commonly used in robberies. The Robbery Profile Form allows police to spend less time interviewing clerks and more time pursuing robbers—with better information to go on.

Clerks are also trained in personal safety off the job. "We want our people to be safe from crime at home as well as at work," Southland's Alisa Martin said. The company provides employees with a booklet of crime-prevention tips and has produced three fifteen-minute videotapes: one on the robbery-prevention program, one on violence prevention in general, and one on rape awareness. Southland makes the tapes available to the public.

As part of its crime-prevention program, the company also offers rewards of up to $25,000 for information leading to the arrest of 7-Eleven robbery suspects. The rewards were originally paid only after conviction, but Johnson persuaded the company to pay earlier to let robbers—and the public—know how serious Southland has become about robbery prevention.

"Reward for arrest," Security Manager Nelson explains, "lets people know that we're committed to getting the criminals off the street.

If an informant has to wait for conviction to collect his money, he's much less likely to come forward."

The reward-for-arrest policy also serves to isolate robbers from their friends. Despite the myth that criminals observe a "code of silence," the fact is, they turn each other in quite frequently and generally feel fatalistic about being turned in themselves. Among criminals, the saying goes, "First to talk, shortest walk" (lightest sentence). As far as 7-Eleven robberies are concerned, the first to talk may also collect a reward *forty times larger* than the take from the average armed robbery.

Southland has also recruited taxi drivers into its crime-prevention program. Like 7-Eleven clerks, cab drivers often work alone late at night in exposed positions in high-crime neighborhoods. As a result, they, too, are frequent robbery targets. The taxi program, called Taxis On Patrol, has created a "buddy system" between cab drivers and 7-Eleven clerks. Drivers are invited to use 7-Eleven parking lots as cab stands. Robbers are much less likely to hit either stores or cabs with other people around. Drivers also get free coffee and use of the stores' restrooms. If cab drivers see suspicious activity inside 7-Elevens—or anywhere—they radio their dispatchers who call the police.

Finally, Ray Johnson promotes the program through the media to let would-be robbers know that holdups at 7-Elevens are simply not worth the risk. He has been interviewed by hundreds of newspapers and magazines and has appeared on as many television and radio programs.

"Crooks read newspapers, listen to the radio, and watch TV as much as anyone else," he says. "They also talk to each other and travel in similar social circles. Every time a 7-Eleven robbery nets less than $30, and every time a criminal hears about the robbery-prevention program, the word gets out that 7-Eleven convenience stores are convenient for everyone—except robbers."

The robbery-prevention program has also achieved an unanticipated side benefit—less violence *around* 7-Elevens. "We used to have problems with people loitering around our stores harassing customers," Southland Field Security Manager Robert Buhrig explains. But the same modifications that put robbers on stage inside the stores have worked outside as well. "With all the lighting, and with the clerks and cabs right there, we've had a lot less trouble."

THE CONVENTIONAL WISDOM RECONSIDERED

The 7-Eleven program is noteworthy not only for its elegance, but also for the fact that it contradicts the conventional wisdom about crime control. It has nothing to do with eliminating the supposed breeding grounds of crime. In fact, it achieved its remarkable success during a period of rising unemployment, when the number of Americans living below the poverty line increased more than 15 percent. The economic condition of minorities deteriorated significantly compared to that of whites, social programs were curtailed, the drug traffic flourished, and television violence reached an all-time high.

By the same token, the program's success cannot be attributed to surer arrest and more severe punishment. It has nothing to do with increased police patrols, improved police response times, tougher judges, longer sentences, new prison construction, or the return of the death penalty.

Finally, the 7-Eleven program in no way relies on retricting the availability of handguns or on arming 7-Eleven employees. During the five-year period when the chain cut robberies and crime-related casualties in half, 10 million new handguns were purchased in the United States. 7-Elevens throughout the country experienced uniform robbery decreases despite significant differences in local and state handgun registration laws and penalties for their use in crime. But armed deterrence by 7-Eleven clerks could not have been a factor because of the Southland weapons ban.

What the 7-Eleven experience demonstrates is the power—and tremendous potential—of crime-control programs based on *secondary prevention.* Ray Johnson, the ex-robber, helped equip 7-Elevens with greater "resistance" to armed robbery. Now other businesses interested in preventing robberies consult with Johnson and Southland security personnel.

"Employee morale has gone way up since the robbery-prevention program started," Security Manager Nelson says. "Our people are much safer."

Resources:

Tidel Systems
2615 East Beltline Rd.
Carrollton, TX 75006
(214) 245–8591

The Timed Access Cash Controller costs somewhat more than the typical retail safe. The company's "Robbery Prevention Kit" costs $12.50. It includes door-frame tape measures, robbery profile forms, TACC decals, and a poster to remind employees of robbery-prevention do's and don'ts.

Corporation Security Manager for Field Operations
Southland Corporation
2828 N. Haskell Ave.
Dallas, TX 75204
(214) 828–7451

This is the office to contact to arrange consultations with Southland security experts, or screenings of the company's videotapes on rape awareness and robbery and violence prevention.

2

How One Detroit Neighborhood
Reduced Its Crime Rate 57 Percent

FROM "MOTOR CITY" TO "MURDER CITY" AND BACK

At first glance, Detroit would appear to be the perfect breeding ground for crime. When auto sales plummeted in the late 1970s, unemployment soared. As many as 350,000 Detroit auto workers were laid off, and the recession in the rest of the country meant depression in Detroit. In some neighborhoods, black teenage unemployment reached 80 percent.

Detroit's recent history also includes violent racial strife. The 1967 riot there, one of the worst in the nation's history, left forty-three persons dead and much of the central city in ruins. Even before 1967, Detroit's white population had been moving to the suburbs, but the riot accelerated the process. About 1.5 million whites lived in Detroit in the early 1960s, but by 1978, their numbers had fallen 77 percent to just 350,000.

Starting in 1970, Detroit's crime rate soared. Burglaries, robberies, and auto thefts rose 62 percent. Heroin addiction also increased dramatically. As heroin became cheap and plentiful, life for many Detroiters became cheap and short. Rival heroin distributors fought gangland-style, and the city's murder rate skyrocketed. The once-proud Motor City became known as Murder City, U.S.A.

In 1971, in reaction to the crime crisis, the overwhelmingly white

Detroit Police Department organized a military-style unit called STRESS, an acronym for "Stop the Robberies, Enjoy Safe Streets." STRESS accounted for only 1 percent of Detroit's police, but in two years, its members gunned down twenty-two people, mostly young black men, giving the Detroit police the highest per capita rate of civilian killings in the nation.

When Detroit's economy fell on hard times, auto workers were not the only ones to lose their jobs. Record unemployment seriously undermined the city's tax base, and in 1978 the Police Department was forced to lay off 1,100 officers, *25 percent* of the force.

Poor, unemployed, and underpoliced, with a recent history of rampant crime, heroin tafficking, civil disorder, and police-community animosity, Detroit would appear to be a fertile seedbed for crime. But from 1978 through 1981, while the FBI reported steady increases in crime elsewhere, Detroit's crime rate held steady and in some formerly high-crime neighborhoods it decreased substantially. In the Crary/St. Mary's neighborhood on the city's northwest side, violent crimes (robbery and rape) declined *57 percent*, and property crimes (burglary, larceny, and motor vehicle theft) dropped *58 percent*.

How did Detroit do it? Both residents and police point to two factors: racial integration of the police force, and implementation of one of the best neighborhood crime-prevention programs in the country.

FROM "THEM" TO "US"

In 1974, when Coleman Young became Detroit's first black mayor, he abolished the STRESS unit and established an affirmative action program to recruit women and black people into the police force. By 1978, 38 percent of the force was black and 18 percent female. The massive police layoff that year was based on seniority, but even after the dust had settled, 24 percent of the force was black and 13 percent female.

Department spokesman Fred Williams says, "Detroit is like a big small town. Once the racial makeup of the police force began to reflect the population, the tensions started to ease. Suddenly, everybody knew someone in law enforcement. The police were less 'them,' and more 'us.' "

Racial integration was a start, but it was not enough. In 1976, Mayor Young appointed a new police chief, William L. Hart, and gave him a broad mandate to reduce the city's crime rate. Hart, a black man and former deputy chief, does not fit the stereotype of the big city police chief. He holds a Ph.D. in education and is quiet and soft-spoken.

While still deputy chief, Hart reviewed a crime-prevention proposal by Inspector James Humphrey, a thirteen-year veteran assigned to the department's Crime Analysis Section. Humphrey argued that despite improved police-community relations, traditional after-the-fact policing could not reduce the crime rate significantly. Even with the most advanced equipment and the best possible response times, once a crime was committed there was little the police could do. Year after year, the FBI reported that the nation's police made arrests in less than 20 percent of reported crimes. Census surveys showed that only half the crimes committed are ever reported, reducing the real arrest rate to less than 10 percent. Humphrey proposed that in addition to the department's traditional "reactive" work, it establish a "proactive" Crime Prevention Section to help Detroiters *organize themselves* against crime. The unit Humphrey envisioned would do more than the public relations work that passed for "crime prevention" in many departments. It would use classic community organizing techniques to help residents unite with their immediate neighbors for greater mutual security. A similar program had worked wonders in a high-crime neighborhood of Philadelphia. Humphrey wanted to try the idea in Detroit.

Deputy Chief Hart was impressed, but his predecessor as chief turned down the proposal. "I figured the idea was dead," Humphrey recalls. But a few weeks after Hart became chief, he gave Humphrey the go-ahead to train a group of crime-prevention officers and find a neighborhood willing to test a pilot program.

Hart shared Humphrey's frustrations with reactive police work. "We used to see policing as a 'War on Crime,' with every officer playing General Patton. But the more we looked and acted like the military, the more we alienated the community, and everyone could see that we weren't reducing the crime rate. There had to be another way. So we stopped ordering heavy armaments. We decided we were no longer at war with anyone.

"All the research shows that most criminals live close to where they commit their crimes. The way to apprehend them is not with SWAT teams, but with friendly communication between officers and the community. The people who really know what's going on are the neighborhood residents. The police are not the most important element in the fight against crime. The citizens are, and always have been. To have any lasting impact on crime, the citizens themselves must take the lead."

Police pleas for "more citizen involvement" were nothing new, but traditionally they meant little more than exhortations to support increased police funding. Hart and Humphrey, however, had something different in mind, a contemporary return to neighborhood self-reliance, the kind of mutual aid that controlled crime before police forces developed in the nineteenth century.

With his first group of crime-prevention officers in training, Humphrey started to look for a target area. "I wanted a neighborhood that was representative of the city, but beyond that, one that saw itself as a community, with a neighborhood organization for leadership and a newsletter for publicity." His initial inquiries produced a few nibbles but no bites. Then, almost by accident, he got a call from Jan Williams, president of the Crary/St. Mary's Community Council.

"WE REFUSED TO MOVE"

Jan Williams, a thirty-nine-year-old former nurse, says she called Humphrey because "we were desperate. Crime had gotten so bad, we were scared of our own shadows." It hadn't always been like that in the Crary/St. Mary's neighborhood on the city's northwest side. Kathy Hoard, a thirty-seven-year-old social worker who lives a few blocks from Williams, laughs when she recalls what the area was like when she and her husband bought their home in 1965. "Burglary was practically unheard of. We had a flimsy little lock on our back door and no lock at all on the garage. For the first few years we felt perfectly safe. But then we had the riot, and the blockbusting began, and things really changed."

Williams also remembers the rapid transformation after 1967. "When we moved here, it was lovely: nice homes, tree-lined streets, well-tended yards, a good place to raise our sons. The neighbors were friendly, and we never thought about crime. Back then, the area was about 80 percent white and 20 percent black. But after 1967 the blockbusters came in and started preying on people's worst fears. They said the black families moving in were destroying property values, and many whites sold their homes at ridiculously low prices. Then, of course, the blockbusters resold those homes to black families at top dollar.

"We didn't believe the blockbusters for a minute. We refused to move. By around 1971 the neighborhood restabilized at about 60 percent black and 40 percent white. It was the same community of nice homes and yards, but the feeling was very different. So many homes had been sold so quickly, we no longer knew our neighbors. Everyone—black and white—felt isolated. It wasn't a 'community' anymore. And in no time, the crime rate went sky-high.

"A group of us got together in 1971 to promote racial harmony. We didn't even have a name for the neighborhood back then, but our landmarks were the Crary School and St. Mary's School, so we called it the Crary/St. Mary's Community Council. The council worked for peaceful integration, but after a few years, it became clear that crime was everyone's number one concern. We had no idea what to do about it. Crime makes you feel so helpless. Many people felt like hostages in their own homes.

"I called the police and eventually spoke with Inspector Humphrey. He said he was looking for a community that wanted to get serious about crime prevention. I wasn't sure what he meant, but I said, 'We're it.' "

"THE POLICE HELP THOSE
WHO HELP THEMSELVES"

From Humphrey's perspective, the Crary/St. Mary's neighborhood was a good area for a pilot program. With 155 blocks and 13,000 residents, it was small enough for his fledgling Crime Prevention Section to handle, but large enough to provide a meaningful test. The 60/40 black/white racial mix was representative, and the area had a broad income distribution, from welfare recipients to the upper middle class. Most dwellings were single-family homes, 75 percent owner-occupied, with 25 percent rental units. Most residents were families with children, but 20 percent were over sixty-five.

In early 1977, Humphrey assigned four crime-prevention officers, two black, two white, to the neighborhood. They converted an unused room in a local church into a police "ministation." In addition to being centrally located, the church was also neutral territory, a place where residents who might have felt alienated from the precinct station could feel comfortable.

When the crime-prevention officers met with the Crary/St. Mary's Community Council, they outlined a program that was quite different from what the council had anticipated. The police said that even with saturation patrolling, they could never "deliver" a safer community. "If you want to reduce your crime rate," they said, "you'll have to take the primary responsibility yourselves. We can provide training and act as consultants, but you'll have to provide the leadership and do most of the work."

The program was to be based on a network of block groups. The council would come up with one person per block who was willing to contact everyone on both sides of his or her street and invite them to a series of meetings. The first meeting would be primarily social. Participants would become better acquainted, exchange addresses and phone numbers, and meet one of the crime-prevention officers, who would describe the training that would take place at subsequent meetings.

Over the next few weeks the officers would train block-group participants in street awareness, home burglarproofing ("target-hardening"), and crime reporting so residents could quickly alert the local precinct to suspicious activity by anyone who didn't belong on the block.

The officers would also provide engraving tools to mark valuables with residents' driver's license numbers for identification in case of theft, and stickers:

WARNING

Operation Identification
All articles on these premises are marked
and recorded with the Detroit Police Department

Finally, officers would visit the homes of those interested and conduct "security surveys," evaluations of potential break-in points, then recommend security hardware.

If the block group maintained at least 50 percent participation after the third meeting, the officers would provide two large metal signs, one for each end of the block:

NEIGHBORHOOD WATCH

Detroit Police Department
Crime Reporting and Operation Identification
in Use by This Block Group

The council members were intrigued, but they had several questions. Wouldn't separate groups for every block be unwieldy? Not at all, the officers replied. If someone attempts a crime on your block, who's most likely to notice? Your immediate neighbors. For mutual aid to develop, everyone in each group should be on a first-name basis with everyone else. The way to promote that is to keep things small.

Why the signs? To let would-be criminals know that the residents are security conscious and not easy targets.

Why the 50 percent participation requirement? To make sure that the block is really serious about crime prevention. Inspector Humphrey explains, "One problem with many police-sponsored programs that call themselves 'crime prevention' is that they don't really do anything. What good are Neighborhood Watch signs if the people aren't trained, don't know each other, and don't take any responsibility? That's tokenism, not crime prevention. Token programs don't work. The crime rate doesn't change, and all that happens is that the Neighborhood Watch concept looks silly. Crime is a tough problem. People *can* deal with it, but they've got to be willing to work."

Chief Hart cites another reason for the 50 percent participation requirement: simple pragmatism. "This department is stretched very thin. We can't fight crime by ourselves. We're only as good as the community is. If a majority of the people on a block aren't willing to take responsibility for their safety, we can't do much for them. We have to deploy a limited number of officers for maximum effectiveness. They're most effective where the people are most organized. Our philosophy is: The police help those who help themselves."

140 BLOCK GROUPS CUT CRIME 57 PERCENT

When the crime-prevention officers first explained the program, the Crary/St. Mary's Community Council was skeptical. They wanted more police patrols, but the officers said that saturation patrolling had been shown to make no difference. Instead, the police threw the responsibility back on the neighborhood.

"We had our doubts," Kathy Hoard remembers, "but the officers had energy and they had *hope*. What they said made sense. It sounded honest and realistic, and everyone agreed that we had no better alternative."

Each community council member agreed to organize a first meeting on his or her own block. "We were all nervous that we wouldn't get the 50 percent," Williams recalls, "but it was a magic number, a goal. I talked to neighbors I'd never met before. Once we started meeting together, the feeling on our block began to change for the better."

On some blocks, the organizing went smoothly. The groups quickly involved more than 50 percent of the families; names, addresses, and phone numbers were exchanged; crime-prevention training took place; and Neighborhood Watch signs were erected. Participants began keeping an eye on each others' homes, and many installed new locks as a result of security surveys. Older people got involved, and many retirees who were home during the day became block leaders. If anyone was unable to install recommended security hardware, their neighbors or the officers helped them.

But on other blocks, the organizing proved more difficult. Some residents were simply not interested. For others, fear and mistrust overwhelmed the urge to participate. "On one block," Williams recalls, "everyone was paranoid. They'd had so many burglaries that nobody trusted anyone else enough to hold a first meeting. Everyone was afraid that someone might case their home for burglary. But at the same time, no one wanted to go anywhere else for the first meeting for fear that their home would get hit while they were gone! That was really frustrating. Finally, we set up a meeting at a local church. To ease the fears of burglary, one officer parked in his patrol car in the middle of their block for the entire evening. Later, after they got better acquainted, the group held meetings in each others' homes." Within two years, 140 of the 155 blocks in the area met the criteria for Neighborhood Watch signs. About 10,000 of the 13,000 residents received crime-prevention training, and the police conducted more than 600 security surveys. Routine police patrols continued unchanged, but crime in the area dropped dramatically:

Type of Crime	1977	1979	Change
Rape	10	4	−60%
Robbery	57	25	−56%
Home Burglary	253	97	−62%
Auto Burglary	99	49	−51%
Larceny	17	9	−47%
Purse Snatching	31	12	−61%

The following year, the Crime Analysis Section investigated the successful burglaries in the neighborhood. The results were striking: *Not one of the burglarized homes participated in Neighborhood Watch.*

Critics of crime prevention often dismiss favorable results by saying that intensive efforts in one neighborhood simply displace crime to surrounding areas, with no net change in criminal activity. To test that theory, the Crime Analysis Section monitored the crime rate in a control neighborhood adjacent to another crime-prevention target area on the city's east side. Crime in the control area *dropped 12.6 percent.* Crime Prevention Lieutenant Norbert Kozlowski said, "If there's any 'displacement effect' from our program, it's displacement of crime-prevention awareness. People see what's working across the way, and naturally they start doing it."

BEYOND SMUGNESS

"After the pilot period," Jan Williams recalls, "we were all proud of ourselves. Actually, we became pretty smug. The crime rate dropped so quickly, people figured we'd licked the problem. The signs were still up, but the energy began to wane. Of course, the signs don't do much by themselves. When the energy level fell, the crime rate inched back up again, not to where it was before the pro-

gram, but enough so that people noticed and realized that they had
to stay involved. Maintenance isn't easy, though, especially when the
key people are all volunteers with other demands on their time."

"You can never completely eradicate crime," Kathy Hoard says.
"You always have carelessness. You always have people moving in
and out, which creates opportunities, and disrupts the block groups.
But when a neighborhood stays organized, you can keep things
pretty much under control.

"The council publishes a monthly newsletter, and every issue,
there's a map showing the exact location of every robbery, burglary,
and auto theft reported two months earlier. Back when the crime
rate was high, many people didn't report crimes. The feeling was,
what's the use? Now everyone understands how important reporting
is. Last year, we had a rash of afternoon burglaries in one corner of
the neighborhood. Everyone saw the clusters of little boxes on the
map. Most burglaries here, especially daytime break-ins, are the work
of neighborhood teens. Sure enough, a man on one of the affected
blocks saw three kids snooping around a house where they didn't belong. He reported it, the kids got caught, and the police found property stolen during the other burglaries in one of their garages."

Since 1979, all 155 blocks in the neighborhood have been organized. Three of the original four crime-prevention officers have been
reassigned to other neighborhoods, and only Nelson Scheuer remains. Scheuer spends much of his time meeting with block groups,
doing security surveys, updating the crime map, dealing with youth
problems, and acting as a liaison between the community and the
city. Just about everyone in the area knows him, and residents affec-
tionately call him "our cop."

"What we've got now," Kathy Hoard beams, "is a sense of community. The neighborhood feels like a small town. Not that people
pry. You can be as involved as you want and still preserve your pri-
vacy. But the community is more cohesive now. We know our
neighbors, the crime rate is way down, and we're not afraid anymore."

4,200 BLOCK GROUPS

The success of the Crary/St. Mary's program was anything but a
fluke. From 1977 to 1981, a similar program in Chandler Park, a

150-block neighborhood on Detroit's east side, reduced violent crime 56 *percent* and property crime 60 *percent.*

Since then the crime-prevention program has gone citywide. Neighborhood Watch groups have been organized in 4,200 of Detroit's 12,000 residential blocks. New block groups continue to be organized, but increasing emphasis has been placed on maintaining existing groups, including a new wrinkle, decertification.

"Block groups are now required to meet with a crime-prevention officer at least once a year," Inspector Humphrey says. "If they don't, we take their signs down. Once the signs go up, people want them to stay there, so decertification helps keep everyone involved. It also encourages old members to reach out to new neighbors; you wouldn't believe how much people move around. Of course, we encourage the block groups to meet on their own more often, and many do, but now every group meets at least once a year. It's crucial to keep reviewing the fundamentals."

Neighborhood-based crime prevention, once an experiment, has become a cornerstone of the Detroit Police Department. Despite the 1978 layoff, the number of officers assigned to Crime Prevention has increased from 2 to 165, most assigned to an expanded network of 50 ministations around the city. The ministations are staffed not only by crime-prevention police, but also by more than 2,000 community volunteers.

Detroit's ministations look more like community centers than police stations. One afternoon, the East Warren ministation, a storefront near the city's eastern border, was bustling. While Officer Robert Adams made arrangements with a local appliance store owner for a security survey, volunteer Kathy Duncan, a school secretary, was on the phone providing referrals to a caller whose neighbor was a victim of domestic violence. Another volunteer, Bill Rinehart, a local bartender, was drawing up the assignment sheet for the forty community residents in the area's volunteer car patrol. Equipped with CB radios, the patrol supplements police patrols on weekend nights. If patrollers spot suspicious activity, they do not intervene directly. They keep the situation under surveillance and radio their dispatcher at the ministation, who calls the local precinct. (The car patrol works in coordination with local cab drivers, who were organized into crime prevention by the area's 7-Elevens.)

"I was skeptical when the ministation opened," Rinehart recalls.

"Everyone was. The police never had the best reputation around here. But I live and work in the neighborhood, and I want to see it kept up. Since the block groups and the car patrol got organized, our crime rate has gone way down."

POLICE "REBORN"

Nelson Scheuer, the 37-year-old Crary/St. Mary's crime-prevention officer, used to feel cynical about police work. "I walked a beat and worked a patrol car and it didn't take long to become very discouraged. This may sound idealistic, but I joined the department to do community service. I never wanted to shoot people or kick doors in, but that's what I wound up doing. When you're a cop, you wind up working with the one percent of people who are misfits, and it's hard not to start seeing the rest of the world that way. You never see the fruits of your labor. Nothing ever changes. It's the same crap, day in, day out. And no one ever says 'Thank you.' Cops often act macho and say it doesn't bother them. But it does. In my case, the strain got worse and worse. I got divorced and transferred to a desk job. Then I joined Crime Prevention, and I've been here ever since. Forget the TV shows; this is what police work is all about. I feel a sense of purpose. We've really accomplished something. Times have been tough here—high unemployment and a depressed economy. But as far as crime is concerned, the quality of life has really improved, and everybody knows it."

In July 1982, the Crary/St. Mary's Community Council planted a twenty-foot maple tree on the grounds of the Crary School. In front of it, on a granite marker, is a bronze plaque in Nelson Scheuer's honor.

Stories like Scheuer's are typical of police who work in Crime Prevention. Detroit's Crime Prevention Section is filled with veterans of tactical mobile units and other "heavy" assignments, who, like Scheuer, decided they preferred community work to busting heads.

"Unlike a lot of cops," Inspector Humphrey says, "our people *like* coming to work. They feel reborn. Neighborhood organizing gives you more control over your life. Reactive policing is so frustrating: You're tied to a radio, dispatched all over, trying to comfort people you can't comfort, chasing people you hardly ever catch."

"I've done just about every kind of police work," twenty-year veteran Lieutenant Norbert Kozlowski says, "and Crime Prevention is the only thing that really makes a difference. Most people want to do something about crime. The same goes for most cops, but you get cynical just mopping up after it. Even when you capture a criminal, it's hard to feel much satisfaction. You're always too late. The damage has already been done. What can you say to the victim? Maybe you put a few crooks away for a while, but the community stays hurt for a long time. Eventually, the criminals get out and go right back to where they used to work, so where are you? Reactive police work can't do anything to break that cycle, but proactive policing can."

In addition to feeling better about their work, Detroit police cite another benefit of crime prevention: fewer police casualties. During the STRESS/War-on-Crime period, Detroit police fought many gun battles with residents, and every year several officers died in the line of duty. But since the department adopted its community organizing strategy, police casualties have declined substantially. Chief Hart says, "Crime prevention has made Detroit safer for everyone."

The Detroit Police Department has by no means abandoned reactive police work. Even with the shift toward proactive efforts, the Crime Prevention Section accounts for only 4 percent of the department's budget. As small as that is, it's *twenty times* what the average police force spends. Inspector Humphrey explains, "The typical department spends just .2 percent on proactive work. A lot of police are stuck in what I call the John Wayne Syndrome. They feel that 'real' police chase after criminals and make arrests. But when you've got a good crime-prevention program, you cut the crime rate and have a lot fewer criminals to chase. Think about it: 99.8 percent of the average police budget goes to the guys who sit around waiting for something bad to happen, while just .2 percent goes for the work that produces the best results. When are people going to wake up?"

THE CONVENTIONAL WISDOM RECONSIDERED

Like the 7-Eleven example, Detroit's crime-prevention experience also contradicts the conventional wisdom about crime control. The Motor City's crime rate plummeted without increased police manpower or funding. In fact, the Detroit police budget has decreased since 1975, and the number of officers has also declined.

Detroit's success also flies in the face of the conventional wisdom about guns and crime. Gun-control advocates argue that "the more guns, the more crime." But in Detroit, the crime rate fell dramatically despite surveys that showed substantial annual increases in gun ownership. Advocates of armed deterrence, on the other hand, argue that guns prevent crime. But armed deterrence has nothing to do with the Detroit program.

Finally, Detroit's crime rate declined despite the city's worst social and economic crisis since the 1930s. Jobs evaporated, welfare rolls swelled, social services were cut back, and most white people left the city.

"If poverty, unemployment, and a large black population cause crime," Lieutenant Kozlowski says, "Detroit should be number one. But we had more crime when the economy was in better shape. What we didn't have was a sense of community. I was like everyone else. I'd lived in my house for years, but I didn't know my neighbors. Then we organized a Neighborhood Watch and now I know them all."

Sense of community. In recent years, many authorities have charted its breakdown, mourned its passing. Some of the grief may be justified, but much of it seems premature.

"We get visitors from all over the world," Lieutenant Kozlowski said. "Everyone wants to see how the program works. They all come away saying, 'If it can work in Detroit, it can work *anywhere.*'"

Resource:

Crime Prevention Section
Detroit Police Department
1300 Beaubien, Room 207
Detroit, MI 48226
(313) 224-4030

Officers may be able to respond to selected inquiries. Publications include numerous crime-prevention pamphlets and the quarterly newsletter, "An Ounce of Prevention."

3

How Much Crime? Who Are the Criminals? Who Are the Victims?

"OUT OF CONTROL": CRIME OR CRIME STATISTICS?

Ask anyone how much crime is committed, and invariably they reply, "Far too much." But the consensus ends there. To analyze the true prevalence of crime, we must use crime statistics. Unfortunately, the two agencies that compile them, the FBI and the Census Bureau, produce contradictory reports.

The FBI asserts that the crime rate soared from the mid-1960s through 1980 and has since leveled off. But the Census Bureau insists that it has been relatively stable since 1973. The media present FBI crime statistics as revealed truth, but many critics insist that the FBI *underestimates* the actual number of crimes by 50 percent. How can crime be "soaring," yet "stable" at the same time? And if the FBI does, in fact, underreport crime, how could the Census Bureau call it *anything but* out of control?

Fortunately, the situation is not as contradictory as it appears. Crime statistics become clearer when viewed historically. Before 1930, the United States had no national crime statistics. Then the International Association of Chiefs of Police recommended the collection of national statistics for seven "index crimes": murder, rape, robbery, aggravated assault, burglary, larceny, and motor vehicle theft. In 1930, the FBI began to compile reports of index crimes in its annual Uniform Crime Reports (UCR).

43

FBI crime statistics may sound authoritative when announced on the evening news, but they are about as reliable as political campaign promises. First, the UCR is a *voluntary* program. The FBI has no authority to compel any police department to participate. In the UCR's first year, 400 police departments reported their crime figures. By 1980, the number had increased to 15,000. As more police departments joined in the program, more crimes were reported. (The FBI also reports the rate of index offenses per 100,000 population, but these figures tend to get lost in media reports of the *number* of crimes.)

In addition to the huge increase in the number of participating police departments during the last twenty years, significant efforts have been made to encourage victims to report more crimes. Most departments have set up 911 numbers and anonymous witness hot lines. The recent proliferation of rape crisis centers, family violence agencies, and victim assistance programs has increased the reporting rates for many crimes. The upshot has been higher UCR crime totals without real evidence that more of these crimes are, in fact, being committed.

Another problem is that more crimes than ever are counted as "real." Before 1973, larcenies were counted only if the loss was greater than $50. Since then, all thefts have been counted. The most frequently reported theft crime is shoplifting, which in most cases amounts to less than $50. Not surprisingly, one of the biggest jumps in the larceny rate in the last fifteen years took place from 1973 to 1974, the first year of the new larceny reporting system. Arson became the eighth index crime in 1978, and contributed to the "sharp increase" in the FBI's overall crime tally from 1978 to 1979.

According to Albert Biderman, a specialist in crime statistics, these problems "inflate the newer figures relative to the older ones . . . and show spurious increases in the crime rate. [The UCR] does not provide a sound basis for determining criminal behavior."

"RELATIVELY STABLE SINCE 1973"

For all these reasons, President Johnson's 1967 Crime Commission recommended the creation of a supplemental crime report, based not on questionable police information but on census surveys of Americans' actual crime experiences. That led to "Criminal Victimization in the United States," a Justice Department publication based on census surveys of 135,000 Americans every six months since 1972. Census victimization surveys are by no means error-free, but authorities agree that they provide more reliable information about crime trends than the UCR. Every year, the census surveys have produced the same two findings: More than half of crimes go unreported; and the crime rate has remained relatively stable since 1973.

Census surveys have shown that underreporting is even more of a problem than had been previously suspected. Only 45 percent of violent crimes and 25 percent of theft crimes are ever reported to police. Some victims fear retaliation if they report. Others decide reporting small uninsured losses "just isn't worth it." Some feel too embarrassed to report, as, for example, a man robbed by a prostitute. Finally, many victims fear inappropriate behavior by police, especially in cases of rape, domestic battering, or incest. Despite these problems, many crimes are more likely to be reported today than ever before, particularly rape. When sexual assault first emerged as an important social issue, most authorities estimated a reporting rate of only 10 percent. But by the 1979 census survey, the figure had increased to about 50 percent. Overall, however, underreporting remains a serious problem that distorts UCR findings.

According to the UCR, from 1973 to 1979, the index crime rate "soared" 46 percent. But during the same period, the census recorded an increase of only about 5 percent. Of course, the relative stability of the census figures is cold comfort when victim surveys show that crime touches *twice as many Americans* as the already-too-high FBI statistics imply, and when independent of the true crime rate, *fear* of crime has clearly risen sharply in recent years.

Nonetheless, the census figures are grounds for cautious optimism. For the past decade, the crime rate has been more stable than the FBI has led us to believe. The crime rate is certainly too high, but contrary to prevailing myth, crime is not "soaring out of control." If we face the problem realistically, as Detroit and the 7-Eleven chain have, we can all become much safer. But to take appropriate action, we need to know more about the criminals we're up against.

THE TARGET, NOT THE TAKE

Who are the criminals? A good deal of fiction, film, and television depicts them as cool professionals who commit their crimes with cunning and skill, even grace. Criminal masterminds do exist. The Great Train Robbery comes to mind, or the occasional six-figure armored car holdup. But how many such crimes do we hear about each year? One or two? Five? By far the most lucrative index crime is bank robbery (average take $2,800 in 1980). But bank robbery accounted for an infinitesimal .02 percent (2 out of 10,000) of the 40 million crimes that year. According to Marcus Ratledge, for twenty years a burglar and auto thief, "The chance of encountering a true professional . . . is about the same as the chance of finding a diamond mine in your backyard."

The major difference between the few professionals and the overwhelming majority of criminals is that the latter pick the target, not the take. They also tend to strike with a minimum of planning. What kind of people are they? Creatures from another planet? It seems that way at times, but the vast majority are rather like the rest of us—only more impulsive and opportunistic.

THE IMPULSIVE OPPORTUNISTS

How do criminals really operate? The best perspectives come from criminals themselves. "We never did no real planning when we were checking out a place to rob," writes former burglar John Allen. "It was like we'd see the place, and if it was easy to get in by climbing a drainpipe or going through a window, we'd do it. Most of the time, it *was* easy." Marcus Ratledge concurs. "Most of those who steal are not willing to take more than minimum risks. They usually steal only what is readily available."

Street criminals are impulsive and opportunistic to begin with, but their life-styles, which typically include abuse of drugs and alcohol, make them even more so. The link between crime and heroin has been widely noted, but the crime-alcohol connection is considerably more important. Only a small fraction of criminals are heroin addicts; many more are heavy drinkers. All intoxicating drugs reduce inhibitions, but few stimulate impulsiveness—and violence—as much as alcohol. "People underestimate the importance of alcohol in crime," one burglar told Charles Silberman, author of *Criminal Violence, Criminal Justice.* "I never went out on even the simplest burglary without a drink under my belt. Make that a few drinks."

A 1979 Justice Department study of prison inmates shows that one-third drank "very heavily" immediately prior to the crimes for which they were imprisoned, and that even those who did not drink heavily said they typically used alcohol prior to committing their crimes. The study concluded that crime had "much more to do with alcohol abuse than had been anticipated."

Another dimension of criminal impulsiveness is that after a "score," they rarely quit while they're ahead. E. H. Sutherland, who interviewed dozens of robbers for his book, *The Professional Thief,* concluded that crimes committed largely on the spur of the moment were typically followed by equally impulsive spending sprees. One mugger says, "A thousand-dollar rip-off means you can relax for a while, right? Oh no! I'd go out, get high, and go through it in three or four days."

Who are these inebriated, live-for-the-moment opportunists? Are they "career criminals" who choose violence and theft the way others choose medicine or law? A tremendous amount has been written about what "causes" crime, but one fact of paramount importance is, quite simply, age. Most criminals are men under twenty-five.

THE YOUNG AND THE RECKLESS

Crime is a young man's occupation. In 1980, 81 percent of burglars, 73 percent of armed robbers, and 54 percent of rapists were men under twenty-five. Because they are young, criminals have limited experience in the world. Like most people, they prefer the familiar to the unfamiliar. As a result, they tend to operate close to home, usually within their own age, race, and ethnic groups. Census surveys consistently show that 80 percent of violent crime is intraracial. And an exhaustive Justice Department study of burglars showed that the "most typical" burglar was a seventeen-year-old boy who struck *less than one mile from home.* Even sophisticated thieves prefer to work close to home. The burglar who shot and killed noted Washington cardiologist Michael Halberstam in 1980 was one of his neighbors in fashionable Georgetown. Police said he had burglarized many homes in the area.

Weapons also play a role in criminal impulsiveness. Psychologists say that criminals beyond their midtwenties tend to use weapons mainly to get the job done, while younger criminals, particularly minority youth, use them to feel like "somebody." They may have heard that "all men are created equal," but in their lives, the only guarantee of equality comes from that great equalizer, the handgun. "If you feel like you're nothing," one said, "a gun can make you feel in total control . . . like playing God."

Criminals may feel "in total control" at times, but as they approach thirty and mature beyond the live-for-today attitudes of younger men, those Godlike moments look increasingly brief and illusory. Past age thirty or so, the criminal life simply loses its appeal as a way to make a living. "You get older," one ex-burglar explains, "and grow out of it."

"THE RETIREMENT PLAN WAS TERRIBLE"

Law enforcement officials are quick to say that "crime pays." Fighting it often pays quite well for them, but does it pay for the working criminal? That largely depends on how old he is. The typical burglar is seventeen. Whether he's black or white, poor or middle class, to a teenager who hits for $900, the average take for reported burglaries in 1980, it certainly looks like crime pays. But not for long.

Arrest rates are low, but eventually all criminals get caught. Most criminals understand this instinctively. Ray Johnson, the 7-Eleven consultant, says, "The police can make a thousand mistakes, but the criminal can make only one." To quote a criminal adage: "Don't do the crime if you can't do the time."

Johnson sums up his crime years this way. "The hours were great. The money, when I had it, was all right. But the retirement plan was terrible. I took in thousands, but my yearly income was at the poverty level. The time I spent actually pulling jobs comes down to maybe a month or two, which got me twenty-five years behind bars. After that, a steady job—any legitimate job—looks pretty good."

The crime life is a grubby, dangerous, high-stress existence. As criminals approach thirty, even the craziest tend to mellow, and in Charles Silberman's words, "make the startling discovery that honest work pays better than crime. To adolescents, crime appears to be easy and well paid. The reality is that few people have the talent to earn a good living at it. One thief remarks, 'It's a hard thing to steal for a living. You're out there every day. And you don't always run into gravy.' "

Stealing for a living also means that your "job" provides no sick leave, holidays, or vacations; no Social Security or pension; no union protections; and possibly most important of all given the serious risks of injury, no health insurance.

Beyond personal maturity the other crucial factor in rehabilitation is marriage. "The most compelling reason for going straight," Silberman writes, "is that young men fall in love, marry, and have children. Marriage and the family are the most effective correctional institutions we have." Ray Johnson is a case in point. While serving his final prison term, he fell in love with a woman who worked in the front office. After his parole, he moved in with her and her children. Despite his difficulties finding work, their support helped keep him straight.

DEMOGRAPHICS: LESS CRIME TOMORROW

Violent crime has always been a fact of life in the United States, but the crime rate itself has fluctuated considerably. We can gain insight into long-term crime trends by focusing on the most violent crime, murder. Homicide has been recorded since Cain slew Abel. U.S. murder records are far from perfect, but since 1900, they have been complete enough to allow historians to construct a reasonable estimate of this century's homicide trends.

From 1900 to 1940, the murder rate skyrocketed. Then something completely unexpected happened—homicides plummeted 50 percent through the 1940s, and overall crime is estimated to have declined by about 30 percent. The murder rate remained low until the mid-1960s, then it rose dramatically through the mid-1970s. It has since leveled off and begun to decline. In 1980, the murder rate stood at about where it was during the late 1930s. If, as H. Rap Brown once observed, "violence is as American as cherry pie," why did the murder rate fall during the 1940s, and why is it falling today?

The most persuasive reason has to do with trends in the nation's birth rate. The birth rate is our best predictor of the murder rate a generation later. Births rose sharply from the late nineteenth century through 1920. As a result, the number of men in their prime crime years, ages fourteen to twenty-four, increased markedly, and the murder rate soared from the turn of the century to 1940. The birth rate plummeted from 1920 to 1935 and remained relatively low through 1945. As a result, there were comparatively few young men in their prime crime years from the mid-1940s through the late 1950s, and the homicide rate plunged. (In addition, a large proportion of the young men in their prime crime years during the 1940s left their communities to serve in the armed forces.)

From 1945 through 1957, however, the birth rate soared to its highest point in U.S. history. The much-chronicled Baby Boom did more than weave Dr. Spock and rock music into the cultural fabric. The "pig in a python" (demographic bulge)—the 77 million Americans born between 1946 and 1964—led to an explosion of crime from the mid-1960s through the late 1970s.

The birth rate peaked in 1957. By 1977 it had fallen to the lowest point in U.S. history. Demographers say the Baby Boom ended with those born in the early 1960s. The first wave of the postwar generation, those born from 1946–1950 and now in their mid and late thirties, are well past their crime years. The second wave, those born 1951–57 and now in their late twenties to early thirties, are emerging from their latter crime years. The third wave, those born from 1956–1964 and now in their late teens to midtwenties, are in their prime crime years. But this final group was born when the birth rate was dropping precipitously. It is considerably smaller than the earlier waves of the Baby Boom.

The implication is that adult arrests from the tail end of the second-wave group should have remained high through the early 1980s, but that juvenile arrests from the smaller third-wave group should have begun to decline. This is precisely what has happened. Although arrests of adults in their twenties remained high through the

1970s, during the latter half of that decade, juvenile arrests *declined almost 19 percent.*

"The official and journalistic view," Florida Juvenile Judge Seymour Gleber writes, "is that juvenile crime is ever-increasing. But in recent years, juvenile crime has declined, a trend that has been evident since the mid-1970s."

Despite the slight upturn in the birth rate since 1977, the Baby Boom generation is having fewer children than its parents did, and the population of fourteen to twenty-four year olds should remain small through 1990. Alfred Blumstein, of Carnegie-Mellon University, writes: "Arrests should peak in 1980, prison commitments in 1985, and the prison population in 1990. The subsequent decline should reflect the maturation of the post-War Baby Boom generation out of the high-crime age group, and later, out of the prison-prone age group."

Of course, demography is not destiny. Although the postwar population bulge is moving into its latter crime years, this does not mean that crime will disappear—far from it. There will always be young men who feel alienated enough to let the combination of impulse and opportunity get the better of them. But the declining proportion of young men in the population is one reason for cautious optimism about personal safety in the coming decade. Another is that the population as a whole is growing older, and despite the fact that fear of crime tends to increase with age, real risk of criminal victimization *decreases.*

CRIME VICTIMS: YOUNG MEN, NOT OLD WOMEN

Anyone might fall victim to crime, just as anyone might develop cancer. But like cancer, crime has many risk factors that influence individual susceptibility: age, sex, race, ethnicity, income, employment, marital status, and place of residence.

Recall that most criminals are young men who operate close to home and target victims of their own race and age. As a result, 80 percent of the crimes reported to census interviewers were intraracial, and young men were at highest risk. Men are assaulted twice as often as women. Those aged twelve to twenty-four have the highest victimization rate, those over sixty-five the lowest. After age twenty-four, victimization decreases with age. Risk also decreases with age, because fear of crime increases and older people take more precautions.

Black people commit a disproportionate number of index crimes. As a result, a disproportionate number of victims are also black. Black men are at highest risk, followed in decreasing order by white men, black women, and white women. Hispanics are more vulnerable than non-Hispanics.

The one exception to the rule that young men target young men is rape. Although rape victims may be any age (and either sex), most rapists and rape victims are under thirty, and most victims share their attackers' race and ethnicity.

Physical location also has a good deal to do with victimization risk. Most robberies take place in "no man's lands": parks, playgrounds, schoolyards, stairwells, elevators, parking lots, and public transportation facilities. The second most frequent location is in or near the victim's home.

Not surprisingly, urban residents are at highest risk, followed closely by suburban residents and, more distantly, by those in rural areas. Among urban and suburban residents, those who live in highest density areas are at greatest risk.

The unmarried, separated, or divorced are at higher risk than the married or widowed. The unemployed are at higher risk than those with jobs.

The income/crime relationship is more complex. On the one hand, the higher the income, the lower the risk of violent crime. High-income people tend to be older, less urban, and more often white, hence lower risk. They also have more discretionary income to finance security precautions. On the other hand, the relationship of income to burglary risk is less pronounced, because young men often experiment with burglary independent of social class, and because affluent homes are more likely to be targeted by older, more skilled thieves from outside the immediate neighborhood.

RATE YOUR RISK: HOW VULNERABLE ARE YOU?

Although it's impossible to assess precisely anyone's risk of criminal victimization, the 1979 census survey provides a sound basis for deriving reasonable estimates. For each group of crimes, simply add the numbers that apply to determine your risk:

RATE YOUR RISK OF VIOLENT CRIMES:

Robbery, Rape, Assault

Age

Age Group	White Male	White Female	Black Male	Black Female
12–15	66	41	75	28
16–19	92	54	68	49
20–24	95	45	99	59
25–34	57	30	62	39
35–49	23	17	36	26
50–64	11	8	25	14
65+	7	4	11	13

Race/Ethnic Group

Race/Ethnic Group	Male	Female
White, non-Hispanic	40	22
White, Hispanic	54	29
Black	53	32
Other	47	25

Income

Annual Income	White	Black
Under $3,000	60	65
$3,000–7,499	41	43
$7,500–9,999	43	43
$10,000–14,999	33	45
$15,000–24,999	30	19
Over $25,000	30	38

Locality of Residence

Locality	White Male	White Female	Black Male	Black Female
City	62	34	66	37
Suburb	45	24	50	31
Other	31	15	27	20

Marital Status

Status	Male	Female
Never married	79	43
Married	24	12
Divorced/Separated	87	68
Widowed	14	8

Education (Age 25 or over)

Highest Level	White	Black
Under age 25	20	30
Elementary		
0–4	14	16
5–7	11	11
8	7	27
High School		
1–3	18	33
4	18	32
College		
1–4	33	50
4+	27	34

Employment (Age 16 or over)

Job Status	White	Black
Under age 16	39	38
Employed worker	39	38
Unemployed worker	71	81
Keeping house	11	32
In school	52	71
Unable to work	13	33
Retired	7	11
Other	42	44

Violent Crime: Rate-Your-Risk Score

Risk Group	Male	Female
Lowest	less than 146	less than 111
Medium Low	146–223	111–168
Medium	224–315	169–222
Medium High	316–400	223–283
High	401+	284+

RATE YOUR RISK OF THEFT CRIMES:

Burglary, Motor Vehicle Theft

Age of Head of Household

Age	Burglary	Motor Vehicle Theft
12–19	222	43
20–34	111	24
35–49	93	21
50–64	64	14
65+	45	5

Number in the Household

Number	Burglary	Motor Vehicle Theft
1	77	12
2–3	82	17
4–5	92	19
6+	97	35

Number of Units in the Building

Number	Burglary	Motor Vehicle Theft
1	76	14
2	105	24
3	95	32
4	125	20
5–9	119	26
10+	90	27
Trailers	147	28

Family Income—Burglary

Income	White	Black
Under $3,000	96	127
$3,000–7,499	88	103
$7,500–9,999	82	126
$10,000–14,999	84	105
$15,000–24,999	70	111
Over $25,000	89	155

Family Income—Motor Vehicle Theft

Income	White	Black
Under $3,000	13	8
$3,000–7,499	11	15
$7,500–9,999	16	21
$10,000–14,999	19	27
$15,000–24,999	17	36
Over $25,000	19	37

Location of Residence—Burglary

Population	Central Area	Outside Central Area
Less than 50,000	—	65
50,000–249,999	108	77
250,000–499,999	111	84
500,000–1,000,000	120	78
1,000,000+	103	80

Location of Residence—Motor Vehicle Theft

Population	Central Area	Outside Central Area
Less than 50,000	—	10
50,000–249,000	19	12
250,000–499,999	23	18
500,000–1,000,000	26	20
1,000,000+	37	20

Theft Crimes:
Rate-Your-Risk Score

Risk Group	Burglary	Motor Vehicle Theft
Lowest	less than 363	less than 56
Medium Low	363–405	57–87
Medium	407–485	88–103
Medium High	486–563	104–132
High	564+	133+

Consider these scores as suggestive. You might have a low risk and still find yourself victimized, or a high risk, yet avoid victimization by taking good precautions. Use the survey simply as a tool to evaluate your baseline risk situation. Then keep your score in mind as you read on.

THE VICTIM'S PERSPECTIVE

The Rate-Your-Risk Survey provides one view of crime risk, but to complete the picture, we must examine how victims *feel* about their experiences. In recent years, most states have established Victim Assistance Programs (VAPs). VAPs do not deal with every victim, only with those who ask for help. A look at the calls received by New York City's Victim Services Agency (NYVSA) in 1981 shows which crimes affected victims the most:

Crime	Men		Women		Total	
	#	(%)	#	(%)	#	(%)
Domestic Violence	63	(2)	4,469	(50)	4,532	(37)
Robbery	1,067	(35)	1,454	(16)	2,521	(21)
Assault	1,007	(33)	708	(8)	2,094	(17)
Burglary	477	(16)	1,290	(14)	1,767	(15)
Harassment	136	(4)	474	(5)	610	(5)
Sex Crimes	26	(.8)	563	(6)	589	(5)
Relative's Homicide	297	(10)	82	(1)	379	(3)
Total	3,973	(100)	9,040	(100)	12,113	(100)

(Percentages are rounded off)

Three out of four calls came from women. This is not surprising, because women are more likely than men to seek counseling in general. Most victims called the NYVSA because of violent crimes, but there were enormous differences in the kinds of crimes that prompted calls. Two-thirds of the men called because of street assault or robbery, but *half* the women called because of domestic battering; overall, violence in the home led to more calls (37 percent) than any other crime. Fear of crime typically focuses on victimization by strangers. But in recent years it has become clear that women are at highest risk of assault in their own homes from the men they live with, not from "criminals" in the usual sense of the term.

THE ODDS ARE IN OUR FAVOR

The very fact that most criminals who prey on strangers are impulsive, intoxicated opportunists, who hit perceived targets with a minimum of planning, gives the rest of us the advantage. The burglar, the mugger, the rapist—these men are not the cool, calculating professionals we see on television, even when they're skilled enough to earn a living from crime. They're more like young children. They grab what's within easy reach, and quickly lose interest if thwarted or distracted. Criminals size up their targets quickly and pass up many more than they select. The key is to prevent them from selecting you. That's what the rest of this book is about.

Resources:

"Crime in the United States"
(The FBI's annual Uniform Crime Reports)
$8.00
The Superintendent of Documents
U.S. Government Printing Office.
Washington, DC 20402
Specify order number 027–001–000–27–1

"Criminal Victimization in the United States"
(The Census Bureau's annual victimization report)
Free (one copy per request)
Distribution Services

The National Criminal Justice Reference Service
P.O. Box 6000
Rockville, MD 20850

Criminal Violence, Criminal Justice
by Charles E. Silberman
1980, 746 pages, $4.95
Vintage Books
201 East 50th St.
New York, NY 10022

An excellent discussion of the sociology of crime.

4

How to Prevent Street Assault, Mugging, and Rape . . . and What to Do if You Can't

AN ETERNITY IN THIRTY SECONDS

Ten years ago, when I was a community organizer in Ann Arbor, Michigan, I spent an evening at a coworker's house in a part of town best described as not the safest. I left to walk home around midnight. It was late and I felt tired and preoccupied. I was not watching out.

But what was there to watch out for? I lived less than a mile away, I knew the neighborhood, and I'd walked the route home literally hundreds of times. It was a warm night, and I strode along on automatic pilot.

I skirted a city park. I had sense enough not to take the shortcut through it alone at night. I turned down a side street that was the next best route. Halfway down the block I noticed that a streetlight was out. The street looked much darker without it.

I spotted the first youth about twenty yards in front of me in the unusual darkness. He had emerged from the park and was crossing the street, apparently approaching me. He looked about sixteen, certainly no more than twenty. He was holding an unlighted cigarette aloft between two fingers. He was not smiling.

When he was about ten yards away, I remember thinking, This could be trouble, then immediately dismissed the idea. Come on,

59

don't be so paranoid, I thought. He's just a kid, there's nothing in his hands except that cigarette, and you're no more than eight blocks from home. What could happen?

"Got a match?" he asked.

I slowed my pace momentarily, then it hit me—this *was* trouble. The vibe was all wrong; his voice quivered. I started to accelerate away from him, but it was too late.

"See this, sucker?" another voice barked from behind me. I jerked around. The voice belonged to a second youth, also in his late teens, but bigger and meaner sounding. He had a handgun. Even in the darkness I could see that the hand holding it was shaking. The gunman pressed the weapon against the small of my back and in a harsh whisper barked, "Your money or your life."

Time stopped. Could this really be happening? Right in my own neighborhood? Impossible. But I could feel cold steel trembling against my spine. The kid in front was already rifling my pockets. This *was* a mugging and the two creeps robbing me were more scared than I was. They were both so jumpy, I thought the gun might go off by accident. I seriously thought I might be killed.

"I'm cool," I said as calmly as I could. "I'm real cool. Let's all be real cool." I produced my wallet and, feeling its bulk, remembered I'd cashed a paycheck and was carrying an unusually large amount of money. Dammit, I thought, just my luck. They had no interest in my credit cards, but the one in front eyed my watch, a gift from my parents.

"It's a cheap piece of junk; runs fast," I lied. "You've got lots of money now. Isn't that enough?"

It was. The one behind me said, "Now run. And don't look back or I'll shoot. Go!"

Yes, sir! I sprinted about twenty-five yards in nothing flat. When I looked back, they were gone. The entire incident had taken no more than thirty seconds.

TRUST YOUR INTUITION

At the time of that mugging, I was twenty-four years old, prime risk age for street assault. Why are young people at such high risk? In part because muggers, almost always young men themselves, tend to select targets of similar age, but also because young people—especially men—are often oblivious to the street around them.

Self-defense authorities universally agree that the most important difference between assault victims and nonvictims is that the latter stay poised and alert and take care to avoid high-risk situations.

"We've arrested thousands of street criminals," New York City Crime Prevention Detective Jack Meeks says, "and they all admit that they look for the easy mark. Not the oldest necessarily, not the weakest, but the easiest, people who look like they're in a fog."

I was not exactly in a fog, but I was preoccupied and clearly not sufficiently wary. As a result, I walked right into a situation replete with risk factors for armed robbery: I was alone late at night; the street was deserted; the streetlight was out; I was in a "boundary area" near a city park; and—the most crucial failing—I didn't trust my intuition. What kind of person is out bumming matches at midnight?

Intuition is crucial to assault prevention. Unfortunately, trust in intuitive feelings runs counter to the rationalism that pervades American culture. We're taught to distrust phenomena that defy conventional explanations. I knew something felt wrong about that kid with the cigarette, and had I run right away, before he and his friend closed in on me, I never would have been mugged. But I didn't trust my feelings. I felt embarrassed about being "paranoid."

To the extent that American culture recognizes intuition at all, it tends to be dismissed as a fringe phenomenon (extrasensory perception) or the special province of women, whom men have always considered the less rational sex (women's intuition). Men have their hunches, but in general give less credence than women to intuition, which may have something to do with the fact that they fall victim to street assault twice as often.

Intuition is *real*. No matter what you think of ESP, it's quite clear that almost anyone can at times acquire valid information from sources science cannot explain. In the case of mugging and rape, however, the role of intuition has been explained. It turns out that street assailants use *their* intuition to select targets who broadcast subtle messages that they're "easy rip-offs."

THAT ASSAULTABLE LOOK

Several years ago, Betty Grayson, a professor of social psychology at Hofstra University in Hempstead, New York, was teaching a course in communication to a group of police officers. Part of it dealt with Grayson's special interest, nonverbal communication. Two officers from Manhattan said they could spot people who looked like potential assault victims. Their "picks" were not simply the aged or disabled, those widely assumed to be most vulnerable to attack. They encompassed a broad range of ordinary pedestrians, but something about them attracted the officers' attention. They would follow them, and sure enough, often see them get hassled or mugged. Others in the class reported similar experiences.

Grayson was fascinated. She asked how the officers picked likely assault victims. They shrugged and replied, "Experience." "Gut feelings." "A sixth sense I've developed over the years." "I know it when I see it, but I can't explain it."

Grayson set out to explain it. "I'm not given to mysticism," she says. "My training told me that these police must have become sensitive to subtle nonverbal cues, presumably the same ones muggers and rapists use."

Grayson set up a hidden camera in New York City and videotaped random pedestrians for about seven seconds each, the time muggers say it takes to size up potential victims. Then she took the tapes to Rahway State Penitentiary in New Jersey where she screened them for a dozen prisoners whose opinions of each one's "assaultability" became the basis for a ten-point scale, from "a very easy rip-off," to "too heavy; I wouldn't mess with that one."

Next, Grayson showed the tapes to a second group of prisoners, all convicted of street assault, and asked them to rate each pedestrian on the assaultability scale. Most agreed that the same people, one-third of those videotaped, were "very easy rip-offs."

"Like most people," Grayson recalls, "I assumed that the elderly would be judged the easiest targets. Some were, but many weren't. I was amazed that about a quarter of the younger men and women were also judged easy prey. The question, of course, was why? I'd been a fan of dance for years, and it seemed reasonable to assume that something about the way they moved made them look assaultable."

Grayson then took her tapes to a choreographer, who evaluated each person's movements using Labanotation, a movement analysis system. The results were striking. Every one of the "easy rip-offs" shared five basic movement characteristics: "First, they had exaggerated strides, either too long or too short. Second was the way they moved their feet. Instead of a flowing heel-to-toe walk, they lifted and placed the whole foot at once, as though they were walking on eggshells. Third, they moved 'unilaterally' not 'colaterally,' that is, they swung the left arm and leg together, rather than the left arm with the right leg. Fourth, their upper bodies moved at cross purposes to their lower bodies; their two halves seemed disconnected. Finally, their arm and leg movements appeared to come from outside their bodies, not from within."

Grayson, and coauthor Morris Stein, a professor of psychology at New York University, write: "The prime difference between assault victims and nonvictims ... revolves around 'wholeness' of movement. Nonvictims have organized movements [that] come from the body center. In contrast, victims' movements come from the body's periphery, and communicate inconsistency." In other words, nonvictims look "together"; victims do not.

Studies show that many assault victims get attacked more than once, which lends credence to Grayson's assertion that they broadcast unconscious signals. "We tend to be aware of the situational factors in street assault," Grayson says, "flashing large bills, or walking alone down dark streets late at night. But we're often unconscious of how we move, which is just as important. I'm convinced that if people understood the movements that invite attack, they could be taught not to walk that way and substantially reduce their assault risk."

THE THREE STAGES OF STREET ASSAULT

Joel Kirsch, a California psychologist and longtime student of the martial art aikido, is one of the many assault-prevention instructors who teach people how to avoid mugging and rape using movement principles similar to those identified by Grayson. He and author/psychologist/aikido master George Leonard developed a brief, intensive, assault-prevention course called the "I.C.A. Method" for the three stages of street assault they identified: invitation, confrontation, and altercation.

Their three-stage analysis is extremely valuable because it recognizes that street assaults don't "just happen." They are, in fact, little dramas that follow a predictable pattern. By understanding the pattern—and the options available during each stage—we are in a much better position to avoid attack, or to respond in ways that minimize injury.

Self-protection advice that ignores the three stages of assault may do more harm than good. Some authorities advise "all-out resistance," and cite statistics that show that "resisters" escape more frequently than "victims." This is true, but *only* for resistance during the invitation and confrontation stages. During the altercation stage, especially if the assailant has a weapon, all-out resistance would be foolhardy and quite possibly fatal. The point is that each stage of an assault presents options for response and opportunities for escape. To work, however, the response must fit the stage. The number of response/escape options diminishes as the assault progresses, which is why intuition is so important: It alerts the potential victim *early*, when countermeasures are most likely to succeed.

THE INVITATION STAGE:
THIS COULD BE TROUBLE

No one consciously "invites" attack, but victims often telegraph signals that tell potential assailants, "I'm an easy mark." On the surface, the entire concept of an invitation stage may evoke one of the most destructive myths about sexual assault, the notion that women "invite" rape, or "ask for it," by, for example, dressing provocatively. Rape education organizations have made a considerable effort to debunk this myth. The idea that women who wear alluring clothing invite sexual assault makes as much sense as saying that men who wear expensive suits invite robbery.

"Rape victims," Joel Kirsch says, "do not 'invite' sexual assault in the sense that they have any desire whatever to be raped. They don't. No one does. But depending on the way they move on the street, they may well telegraph their vulnerability.

"Grayson uses the phrase 'wholeness of movement.' In aikido, we call it 'moving from center,' or *hara*. *Hara* is Japanese for the body's center of gravity, a point an inch or two below the navel. When you consciously move from your center, your stride becomes more balanced and whole. You look solid, hard to knock down. But if you move from anywhere else, you literally become a pushover."

In addition to the five movement characteristics which convey assaultability, Kirsch adds that a fixed gaze up or down implies preoccupation, and that a slow stride relative to other foot traffic also tends to attract assailants' attention. It all boils down to looking distracted. Sifting through a purse, staring at the sidewalk or up at buildings, listening to music through a portable cassette player, or reading a map—anything that suggests preoccupation—marks a person as assaultable.

"Acting distracted is a big reason why tourists often get mugged," Kirsch says. "They give off signals that say they don't fit in. The combination of wearing a camera, wandering into high-risk areas, and looking at everything except the street around them makes them magnets for muggers. Also, tourists often carry more valuables than locals."

The best places to find targets, one mugger says, "are hotels, shopping malls, tourist attractions, and hospitals." Hospitals attract muggers because visitors tend to be preoccupied with thoughts of sick relatives or friends. The last thing they expect is a mugging, hence their vulnerability.

Older, more experienced muggers tend to avoid residential neighborhoods because the population density is generally lower than in hotel/tourist neighborhoods, and because local people don't carry expensive cameras and jewelry. Younger, more impulsive muggers, on the other hand, prefer residential neighborhoods or the shopping areas near them. They watch people leave banks or stores and often target those loaded with packages. Then they follow them home and pounce when victims are momentarily preoccupied with their keys.

MOVE LIKE A CAT—BALANCED AND CENTERED

Size, weight, sex, and age are certainly factors in target selection, but they are *considerably less important* than most people believe. Anyone can project an image that says, "I'm not a target." Muggers and rapists generally size up potential victims in no more than ten seconds. You don't have to be big and tough to dissuade them. The trick is to move like a cat: alert, purposeful, and determined. That means walking from your center with a steady, confident stride. It may help to imagine that you are a dancer or a tiger. Look ahead of you. Try not to become too focused on specific objects, especially if it means staring up or down and losing touch with the street around you. Scanning the big picture prevents unpleasant surprises.

Swing your arms comfortably. Try not to keep your hands in your coat pockets; this interferes with wholeness of movement. Many people have cold hands and habitually keep them in their pockets. The cold-hands problem increases with age, as the skin loses some of its insulating ability. From a street safety perspective, it's better to wear light gloves, even if it feels a bit strange at first, than it is to walk with your hands in your pockets. Try this simple experiment. Walk a few blocks with your arms swinging and project a purposeful, don't-mess-with-me feeling. Then try the same thing with your hands in your pockets. Most people find it considerably more difficult to project strength and confidence with hands held close to the body.

BEYOND A CONFIDENT STRIDE

Some of the suggestions that follow may seem obvious, but because street crime is something we generally prefer not to think about, many people ignore them and wind up in trouble. Try not to dismiss them as too simple and don't become intimidated by the size of this list. Simply consider these suggestions, then select the ones that help you feel safer.

• *Try to stay in good physical condition.* You need not become a marathon runner; just try to stay reasonably fit, trim and limber. Fitness lifts the spirits, adds spring to the step and contributes to wholeness of movement. It broadcasts that you take good care of yourself and implies that you can take care of yourself on the street. Of course, exercise should be matched to individual interests and health situations. How you exercise doesn't matter; what matters is that you enjoy doing it regularly. Authorities recommend at least three twenty-minute sessions a week. You need not push yourself very hard. Older people can get good exercise simply by stretching and practicing nonvictim walking.

• *Whenever possible, walk accompanied.* A study by the San Francisco organization, Community United Against Violence, shows that walking with one other person reduces assault risk 67 percent, and that two or more companions reduce it 90 percent. Sometimes it may be inconvenient to recruit friends to accompany you, but if those you know are concerned about street safety, you might arrange schedules to run errands in groups.

In recent years, many police departments, often in conjunction with senior citizens organizations, have established "senior escort services" to accompany older people on errands. These programs have been remarkably successful in reducing street assaults on the elderly. The senior escort program in San Francisco's Tenderloin district shows what a difference walking with another person can make. The Tenderloin is a low-income, high-density neighborhood with a large elderly population. It also has the city's highest rate of street assault. After a rash of assaults on the elderly, the SFPD Crime Prevention Division teamed up with Tenderloin seniors' organizations, and trained two dozen young adult escorts in street awareness. Since the program's inception, Tenderloin seniors have been escorted on more than 180,000 walks around the neighborhood, and *not one* has ever been assaulted.

Other escort programs have organized seniors into "buddy groups" by blocks or buildings. Such groups not only minimize assault risk, but like most self-help programs, they also alleviate loneliness and nurture feelings of personal power, which improve participants' quality of life beyond the programs' crime-prevention focus.

Another way to walk accompanied is to own a dog. Large dogs make excellent attack-deterring companions. Of course, they also have their drawbacks. They demand considerable care, are noisy, and may strain relations with neighbors, who are an important component of any effort to become safer. Nonetheless, if your risk of violent crime is high, a large dog can mean the difference between paranoia and relative peace of mind.

• *Use alcohol sparingly.* Intoxication is a key risk factor for street assault. Alcohol and other drugs distort perception, interfere with intuition, impair reaction time, and disrupt wholeness of movement.

• *Make every effort to walk in populated, well-lighted areas.* Bystanders may not rush to the assistance of those involved in street confrontations, but their mere presence deters muggers and rapists.

• *Whenever possible, park on the street, not in parking garages, unless attendants park and return your car.* Street parking increases risk of auto burglary and theft, but protect yourself before you protect your property.

• *Stay alert while waiting for trains, buses, and elevators.* Many people focus on the approaching public transportation vehicle by scanning the railroad tracks, the street, or looking at the elevator floor indicator. Try to stay aware of the area immediately around you. Then don't enter any vehicle if you sense trouble. There's nothing to feel embarrassed about. Cultivate your intuition, and trust it.

• *Don't hitchhike.* Even if you hitchhike with another person, you're still at considerable risk.

• *In urban areas, have keys in hand before you reach your car or building.* If anyone hanging around makes you uncomfortable, don't enter; walk on and return later. Then, when all seems clear, glance around before you unlock anything. "Push-in" rapes and robberies are quite common.

• *Dress in clothing that does not prevent free movement or running.* Avoid conspicuous jewelry. Women's fashion designers—as well as fashion-conscious women—need to become more aware that few things interfere with fluidity of movement as much as high heels and restrictive skirts.

"High heels," Joel Kirsch says, "raise the center of gravity and put women off balance. They also reduce stride length and wholeness. Tight skirts have similar effects. And if a woman is approached by a mugger or rapist, high heels and tight skirts definitely limit escape and resistance options."

Fortunately, today's fashions encompass a wide range of possibilities, and increasing fitness consciousness has popularized running shoes and active wear. These trends are good news for safety-minded women.

• *If you carry a purse, shoulder-strap models are best.* Walk with the flap side against your body and hold the base of the strap. You might consider trying to get by without a purse, perhaps using jacket pockets, or keeping your valuables separate from other purse items. Another possibility is a backpack; it's difficult to snatch away, and it has the advantage of leaving both arms free.

• *When in doubt, walk in the street—on the left side, facing traffic—not on the sidewalk.* Street assailants depend on surprise; they want to "get the drop" on you. The shadows created by alleys, doorways, staircases, and trees provide cover that attackers use to startle their victims. When you walk in the street, however, the advantage shifts in your favor. Streets are often better lighted than sidewalks. You have greater visibility, and you are more visible to others. The expanse of the street also gives you more room to maneuver and/or run if necessary. Walking in the street, in effect, follows the 7-Eleven guidelines for robbery prevention. It puts the assailant on stage.

• *In high-crime areas, drive with your windows closed and your doors locked.* This prevents anyone from snatching a purse or jumping in when you stop at lights or stop signs.

• *When traveling, ask friends or hotel personnel about areas to avoid.* No matter whether it's an unfamiliar city or a tropical island that seems like paradise, tourists are magnets for street assailants. Tourist publications rarely mention high-risk areas; they don't want to discourage visitors.

• *Finally, give yourself permission to be impolite and "overcautious."* You're under no obligation to smile at everyone, give strangers change or directions, or slow your pace when someone tries to attract your attention. If your intuition registers discomfort, speed up, cross the street, turn around, or do whatever you feel is necessary, then move in a purposeful, determined manner. You might feel you've misjudged someone now and then, but better a little jumpy than jumped.

REASONABLE RISK

One of the most frustrating aspects of working to avoid assault is that preventive suggestions are never foolproof. Even the most consistent and elaborate precautions may not prevent every attack. Self-defense authorities say that nonvictim walking combined with the advice above should reduce assault risk 50 to 90 percent, but some risk always remains.

Another problem is that it's often impossible to take all the precautions you think you should every time you go out. The good news is you don't have to. Most areas don't require "red alerts." You can't eliminate all risks, but you *can* learn to size up street situations quickly, then decide for yourself which self-protection measures feel most appropriate. Mix and match your risk factors and precautions. Intoxication clearly increases risk, but walking with several companions substantially reduces it. You might make a point of staying sober if you know you'll have to walk home alone. But you might allow yourself an extra drink if you know you'll be accompanied by two friends. There's no reason not to wear high heels and carry a purse at business meetings, but you might change shoes and zip your purse into a backpack before leaving work.

Constant paranoia is counterproductive. It interferes with projecting a confident, nonvictim image. The best strategy is to stay alert, recognize risk situations early, and balance them against appropriate precautions.

THE CONFRONTATION: THIS *IS* TROUBLE!

None of the foregoing means that all assault victims are daydreamers who "ask for it." Many careful people suddenly find themselves cornered, with switchblades pressed against their jugulars. What then? Self-defense experts make three basic recommendations:

• *Don't panic.* Try to remain as calm and centered as possible.

• *Assess your risk of physical injury; then if possible, try to take some control of the situation.* Assert yourself up to but not beyond the point where you risk getting hurt.

• *Try to distract or confuse the assailant; then, if possible, run.*
In *The Silent Pulse*, George Leonard summarizes the psychological research on an important, but little-noticed phenomenon, the "holding mechanism" that operates between people who come into close proximity. Figuratively similar to gravity, the holding mechanism subconsciously directs our attention toward those who approach us. A mugger or rapist needs to capture and hold the potential victim's attention long enough to define himself as "the attacker" and his target as "the victim." The outcome of an assault often depends on a split second, the moment of confrontation, when the assailant uses the holding mechanism to attract the potential victim's attention. During the confrontation, the victim nonverbally signals that he or she has been "captured." The confrontation stage does not last long. It's that crucial moment when uneasiness ("This could be trouble.") becomes panic ("My God, this *is* trouble!"). Assailants depend heavily on the confrontation moment; it produces the paralysis they need to transform "persons" into "victims."

When self-defense authorities counsel "resistance," they do not mean starting to struggle once the gun is firmly wedged under your jaw. They mean that if you can't prevent an assault at the invitation stage, try to prevent its progression to the confrontation stage by resisting the pull of the holding mechanism. "The worst strategy," Kirsch and Leonard write, "is to give in to the victim mentality at the moment of confrontation, the belief that 'this guy's a mugger and he's got me.' "

Instead, they recommend trying to break the holding mechanism, a process that feels like waking yourself from a bad dream. First, recognize the subtle force it exerts, then move quickly to overcome the natural tendency to freeze when in danger. Resisting the holding mechanism shows that you are not "ready" to be mugged or raped. You are much less the victim, and you remain freer to maneuver and escape.

Studies show that rape victims recall physical and emotional paralysis during the first few seconds of their assaults; they feel caught, which defines them as victims. Women who have successfully escaped rapists, on the other hand, recall becoming furious and acting on their rage by screaming or running. One analysis showed that 69 percent of women who screamed and 75 percent of those who ran escaped successfully without being raped.

The best way to break the holding mechanism is to scream. Screaming startles the attacker and tends to free the intended victim from the paralysis on which the assailant depends, just as screaming during a roller coaster ride alleviates the fear that may become overwhelming if one remains silent. One study showed that screaming (or using a noise-making device) immediately broke off one-third of impending street attacks, and attracted assistance in two-thirds of cases.

Some authorities make a point of advising those in tight spots to yell "Fire!" instead of "Help!" or "Rape!" because the former is supposedly more likely to summon help. Perhaps, but summoning help is not the main purpose of screaming during the confrontation stage. No matter what you yell, many assaults happen so quickly that even the speediest, bravest good Samaritan might arrive too late. The real purpose of screaming is to break the holding mechanism between you and the attacker. A good bloodcurdling scream may well startle the assailant and, at the same time, fortify your courage to resist further or run. Screaming during a street confrontation might best be compared with the battle cries that armies from time immemorial have used to brace themselves and unnerve their adversaries at the start of attacks.

What you scream doesn't matter; it's *how* you scream. The ideal street scream should sound like the cry of an injured child, so piercing, so intense and bestial that no one within earshot can ignore it, least of all the assailant. In fact, screaming any recognizable word, like "Fire!" or "Help!" reduces a scream's emotional impact, because words automatically impose the rationality of language on an act that draws its power from its very irrationality. Bloodcurdling screams, however, are not as easy to produce as most people think. One hallmark of effective self-defense courses is training in screaming.

"Confuse the enemy" has been a time-honored military strategy ever since the Greeks tricked the Trojans with their wooden horse. Street assailants may not be maniacs, but they are by no means rational or relaxed. Even when armed, they tend to be as scared as their victims; when unarmed, often more so: "I'm always scared," one mugger admits, "scared like the showman before he goes on stage." Muggers and rapists expect the assault to proceed in a certain manner. If, during the confrontation stage, something unanticipated occurs, the assailant's own fears may stop him. Distracting attackers as they move toward you takes advantage of *their* fears and helps break the holding mechanism.

Aikido master Terry Dobson, author of *Safe and Alive*, writes that it may be possible to break the holding mechanism "by doing the weirdest, most unexpected thing you can think of. Fall down, vomit, fake unconsciousness, insanity, epilepsy or heart attack. [These] can be very disconcerting. They are not pleasant alternatives, but they have been known to work in certain situations." Acting bizarre not only helps break the holding mechanism, it may also attract bystanders who might not rush to stop a mugging, but who would aid someone they thought was having a heart attack. Once you break the holding mechanism, *run*.

THE ALTERCATION: HOW TO FACE A WEAPON

If you cannot prevent an assault during the invitation or confrontation stages, you may wind up at the wrong end of a gun, knife, or lead pipe. This is by far the most terrifying aspect of any assault. A weapon means the threat of sudden death, and the memory of facing one lasts a lifetime.

Not all assailants use weapons, but about two-thirds do. FBI data show that 40 percent of armed robbers used firearms; 13 percent, knives; 9 percent, other weapons, for example, blunt instruments; and 38 percent, no weapon. Firearms are the most deadly weapons. When fired, they are three times more likely to kill than other weapons. However, guns are fired much less frequently than other weapons are actually used, and the risk of nonfatal injury is much higher when the assailant has a knife or blunt instrument. Census surveys show that weapons-assault victims who were not killed sustained nonfatal injuries in 17 percent of gun assaults; 28 percent of knife attacks; and a staggering 52 percent of assaults with "other weapons." Why do "other weapons" place victims at greatest risk of nonfatal injury? In part because of the inherently greater risk of death from guns and knives, but also because, as census analysts conclude, "People are less likely to resist when facing more lethal weapons, and resistance invites injury." They should have said, "Resistance *during the alteration stage* invites injury."

Once an attacker "has" you, self-defense authorities advise the course of action shown to reduce injuries in the 7-Eleven robbery-prevention program:

• Remain as calm as possible.

• Do not make any sudden movements.

• Never risk your life for the sake of money or property.

• Give the robber what he wants as quickly and smoothly as possible.

• Concentrate on getting a good description.

• Attempt countermeasures *only* if you are convinced that your life is in imminent danger.

• In rape situations, remain focused, and wait for any moment when the rapist's guard drops, or when his weapon is not on you, then decide whether fleeing or fighting might succeed.

These recommendations are widely endorsed, but if push comes to shove, you must decide for yourself how to respond. There is really only one criterion: *Anything that saves your life and minimizes injury is the right thing to do.*

The problem is that even when doing your best to follow the recommendations above, it's not always clear how to proceed, especially when trying to judge death threats, which are the rule in robberies, muggings, and rapes. These suggestions should help you "manage" assaults that reach the altercation stage:

• *If the attacker has a visible gun or other weapon, take every threat as the word of God.* Don't argue; just do what the man says. But stay focused and continue to look for opportunities to alter the course of the attack.

• *If the attacker SAYS he has a weapon, but does not show it, you might ask to see it.* "This may seem unthinkable," writes karate instructor Judith Fein, author of *Are You a Target?* "but many women get raped by men with nonexistent weapons." A study by Menachim Amir, one of the nation's foremost authorities on sexual assault, estimates that rapists who claim to have weapons, display them only about 20 percent of the time. In other words, in up to four out of five cases, there may not be a weapon. Of course, this suggestion must be balanced against your intuitive sense of the situation.

• *Look at the person, not at the weapon.* When facing any weapon, the tendency is to become transfixed by its power to inflict harm. But as Terry Dobson writes:

By itself, the weapon can't do anything; your problem is not with the weapon, but with the person who holds it. (Try to) make and maintain eye contact (with the assailant). Speak quietly and reassuringly. Try to calm and soothe him by providing assurances that he has nothing to fear from you. This is especially important for someone under the influence of drugs or alcohol.

Another aspect of reacting to a weapon involves sizing up its range. Guns have tremendous power over considerable distances. Recall that guns are used in about 40 percent of armed robberies. This figure is frightening, but it shows that in most robberies guns are *not used.* Knives and blunt instruments are more common than most people think. They can certainly be lethal, and should be taken quite seriously, but their range of effectiveness is smaller, which may increase your options. But remember, the inherent limitations of nonfirearm weapons may increase the assailant's willingness to use them to keep you in the victim role.

Despite the general recommendation to obey an armed assailant, there are times when you might reasonably decide otherwise. Refusal increases your risk of injury, and possibly death, but the decision is yours. It's often prudent to resist being tied up. Once bound, you have no options; you are totally at the assailant's mercy. You might also consider refusing to get into a car if the assailant seems set on taking you to a more secluded location; risk of serious injury increases with seclusion.

If you refuse an order from an armed attacker, avoid direct statements like "Absolutely not; I won't do that." Outright refusals close off options, and should be used only as last resorts. Two other approaches provide more room to maneuver:

• *Negotiation.* Talk with the assailant. Try to keep him talking as long as possible. Despite the fact that his weapon gives him ultimate control, the longer the conversation continues, the more options you gain. In the gunman's eyes, you become less a victim and more a person. Enlightened police departments use negotiation routinely when faced with gunmen/hostage situations. When negotiating,

•

speak as calmly as you can, but try not to plead. Pleading only rein-
forces his power over you. As we have seen, armed robbers prefer to
take the money and run. Give the man your money, but you might
ask to keep your driver's license and credit cards.

Statistically, the older the armed assailant, the more likely he is to
think in terms of robbery, than rape. Many rapists are experienced
armed robbers, with an added dimension of tremendous rage at the
control they imagine women have over them. Rape is a crime of violence, not sex. Most rapists do not primarily want intercourse but
power. They want to degrade and humiliate their victims. Rapists
tend to feel terribly lonely and isolated, in effect ignored by women.
Successful negotiation in potential rape situations often hinges on
redirecting the rapist's attention away from his rage toward his loneliness. Some women have escaped rape attempts by feigning interest
in the man, for example, by offering to fix him a drink while he "re-
laxes" in the living room, then running out the back door. Others
have escaped by saying they're having their period or being treated
for VD, and could they make a date for another time? One California woman arranged a subsequent rendezvous with a rapist, and
when he arrived, she was there—with the police.

• *Distraction.* Recall that distraction can break the holding mechanism during the confrontation stage. It might also work during the
altercation. Attempting to distract an armed assailant means taking a
definite risk, but if he already seems intent on harming you, you may
decide you have nothing to lose.

The inherent disadvantages of an unarmed pedestrian in an altercation with an armed assailant have prompted many people to look
for ways to feel safer. The two most popular approaches are self-defense classes and carrying weapons.

A SHOPPER'S GUIDE TO SELF-DEFENSE TRAINING

Once the exclusive province of the police, the military, and martial arts schools, self-defense classes are now offered to people of all
ages in an enormous variety of settings: Y's, community colleges,
churches, and senior and recreation centers. Should you take a self-
defense class? That depends.

No form of physical training ever made anyone invulnerable to assault. Even the best martial artist can get hurt or killed. One of my karate instructors, a tournament champion, was stabbed to death during a street assault (apparently because he momentarily took his eyes off the assailant during the confrontation stage). When discussing the martial arts, the very term "expert" must be reexamined. My longtime karate teacher told our class over and over again, "A black belt is a beginner." So forget Bruce Lee. Forget every example of martial arts wizardry you have ever seen on television or in the movies. They are fantasies. Even lifelong karate students cannot execute many of the moves that punctuate kung-fu films, and even if they could, Hollywood's flying spin kicks rank among the *least* effective responses to threats of street violence.

Learning how to fight can help a person feel safer, but fighting skills are not as important as most self-defense beginners believe. The best self-defense programs place greater emphasis on sensitizing people to the invitation and confrontation stages of assault, where countermeasures are most effective. Self-defense has less to do with "kicking ass" than with street awareness. People always ask martial arts practitioners, "Have you ever used it on the street?" Those who have progressed beyond Bruce Lee fantasies reply, "Of course, I use it all the time. That's why I don't get into situations that could become violent."

No self-defense program is best for everyone. There are as many good approaches as there are teachers. All self-defense styles are based on similar principles: physical fitness, observation skills, confrontation prevention, and balanced, centered reactions to situations that cannot be avoided. But even instructors who teach the same art—judo, karate, aikido, whatever—interpret it differently and emphasize different skills. One of my teachers, a man with short legs, stressed blocks and punches; another, with long legs, emphasized kicks. *What* is taught is less important than *how* it's taught—and how you feel about the experience. Shop around. Get recommendations. Observe several classes. Select an instructor whose personality and teaching style appeal to you. It's pointless to force yourself to study with an intimidating instructor simply because he or she is a tournament champion. If a self-defense class is part of your personal crime-prevention program, consider it a long-term investment. In this context, the best teacher is someone who could become a friend.

The various martial arts—and all the westernized self-defense styles derived from them—are not separate entities. They are points along a continuum that runs from the "soft" styles to the "hard" ones. Tai chi, a popular soft style, is an elaborate series of choreographed movements. It involves neither sparring nor self-defense techniques applied to street situations, but is based on the same principles as the harder styles, and it produces similar results. It stretches and tones the muscles and focuses the mind. Aficionados often describe it as "a meditation through movement." Because tai chi is gentle and noncombative, it is available to people who would be physically unable to study the more fight-oriented styles. In China, literally millions of people, from children to the elderly, practice it every morning as a wake-up exercise.

On the opposite end of the spectrum are the hard styles, typified by the many forms of karate. Like the soft styles, karate students learn choreographed routines called *katas* (KAH-tahs) that combine the basic blocks, punches, and kicks in meditative dances. They also learn self-defense techniques, short combinations of the basic moves to deal with street attacks. Finally, the more advanced students spar. Sparring partners usually wear padding—arm, shin, and mouth guards—and all blows are supposed to be "pulled" to avoid injuries. Nonetheless, injuries are by no means rare, especially among tournament fighters.

Between the soft and hard styles are many others: for example, judo, best compared with wrestling; and aikido, an increasingly popular style that largely eliminates tournament sparring in favor of self-defense techniques. Aikido is one of the less combative martial arts. It emphasizes parries and throws instead of punches and kicks. The goal is not to obliterate the opponent, but rather to "restore harmony" by defusing the conflict.

As attractive as the martial arts are to some people, to many others they take too much time and discipline, especially if you're impatient to feel safer quickly. In that case, you might try a short-term street-skills workshop. Most of these workshops incorporate aspects of the martial arts, but in abbreviated form, and emphasize street awareness over "punching the guy's lights out." I've taken several one-day self-defense courses and have found them useful and enjoyable.

One word of caution about self-defense training: Bear in mind that the typical street assailant is a man fifteen to twenty-nine; therefore, it's best to take a class where at least some of your practice opponents are men in this age group. Some women's self-defense programs pit female students against one another. This approach has considerable value, particularly as a first class for women who have never punched or kicked, who may be intimidated by the very thought of self-defense. But I've heard women come away from woman-on-woman classes saying, "I can defend myself against women, but I don't know about a rapist." If you decide to study self-defense, it makes no difference how you begin; a woman-on-woman class is fine. But it's best for a woman to move on to courses that include men in the street-assailant age group.

Most self-defense students expect workouts to exercise the limbs, but another part of the body is more important, the larynx. As mentioned earlier, a bloodcurdling scream can break the holding mechanism and allow you to escape before the assailant "has" you. Early in my karate training, the instructor drilled me in *keai*, the martial arts battle cry, until my throat was raw. What a waste, I thought. I came to learn streetfighting and all I'm doing is yelling. I already know how to yell; who doesn't? I soon realized, however, that developing an effective scream requires as much concentration and practice as any other aspect of self-defense training. Screaming is embarrassing. People tend to hold themselves back, which is why practice in letting it all out is so important. One sign of a comprehensive self-defense class, in my opinion, is a training emphasis on effective screaming.

Self-defense training rarely works miracles, but it heightens street awareness and goes a long way toward replacing gnawing paranoia with specific skills for dealing with definable risks. It is especially useful for people whose first reaction to street threats is to assume a victim role.

WEAPONS: TO CARRY OR NOT TO CARRY

Ten years ago, sales of Mace, the tear gas available in a pocket-sized container, were negligible. Today, tear gas sales are estimated at $40 million a year. Mace is merely one of many personal safety tools: police whistles, shriek alarms, skunk odor vials, guns, knives, and clubs. Should you carry any of these? And if so, which?

• *Handguns.* Opinion is passionately divided on the advisability of firearms for protecting one's home, but neither police nor self-defense authorities recommend handguns as personal safety tools on the street. Possession of a loaded gun outside the home is illegal in many parts of the country without a special permit that may be difficult, if not impossible, to obtain. If you carry a gun illegally, you risk criminal prosecution. Even if you have a permit, to use a gun effectively against an attacker you must produce, aim, and fire it, all of which takes time. Your assailant might be faster. If so, he might disarm you and use your weapon against you. If you shoot an attacker, there is no guarantee that the legal system will support you. Laws governing gun-related injuries vary from state to state, but in many parts of the country people who fatally shoot street assailants (or burglars) may be held liable for manslaughter unless they can convince the district attorney (or a jury) that their lives were in clear, grave, and imminent danger. If you shoot and hit anyone, you face almost certain prosecution. Finally, possession of a weapon with such awesome power may create a false sense of security. If carrying a gun makes you feel cocky or less sensitive to potential problem situations, you are more likely to walk into trouble.

• *Tear Gas.* Laws governing tear gas vary widely from state to state. In some states, it's illegal; in others, training and licensing are required; and in some there are no controls. Check with your local police department for the law in your area.

I took a tear gas class and am licensed to carry the two types now marketed for assault protection: CN (Mace), an eye irritant that stimulates the tear ducts and interferes with vision and balance; and the more potent CS, which interferes with breathing and causes asthmalike reactions. The three-hour $45 class was held at a YMCA and included a ten-shot canister of CS. Several of my thirty classmates had been assaulted, and virtually everyone knew someone else who had been. The teacher, a woman karate instructor who taught self-defense at a local college, ran through the state-required curriculum, administered the multiple-choice test, and gave us each an opportunity to "shoot" a dummy. I enjoyed the class, and for a few weeks carried my CS canister in my jacket pocket with the "safety" off. Then I began to wonder.

Tear gas has a number of drawbacks: You must hit the assailant squarely in the face, preferably across the bridge of the nose so the chemical gets into the eyes where it's most effective. Contrary to most people's expectations, tear gas is not a wide-spray aerosol; it's more like shooting a water pistol. Most of the class, myself included, in a completely unpressured situation with good visibility and plenty of time to aim, had difficulty hitting the face, let alone the eyes, of the stationary practice dummy. In a real assault in low light, with a moving target and only a few moments to react, would it work?

I soon learned I was not the only one to wonder about the effectiveness of tear gas. In April 1981, in cooperation with the ABC television program "20/20," the Ventura County, California, Sheriff's Department (VCSD) arranged a unique experiment to test it. Producers Glenn and Karen Winters invited twelve Los Angeles women, all licensed to carry tear gas, to participate in a realistic simulation of street assault, with VCSD deputies playing the assailants.

Lieutenant Steve Giles who arranged the simulation recalls, "We set up a parking-lot situation at the Sheriff's Academy, gave the women shopping bags, and told them to imagine that they were leaving a supermarket. Each carried her usual type of tear gas, either CN or CS. Both the women and the deputies were of average height and build; in fact in some cases the women were bigger than the deputies. The women had the tear gas in their hands with the safety off. They knew something was going to happen, but not exactly what or when. We had diversionary activities going on—kids playing, people walking into the 'market,' a guy changing a tire—so that they wouldn't just spray the first person who crossed their path. Then a deputy posing as an assailant confronted each one and attempted to grab her purse or push her to the ground. Each woman was 'attacked' four times, for a total of forty-eight simulated assaults."

How many did the tear gas stop? Giles says, "Not one."

The women, Giles recalls, "were absolutely convinced the tear gas would work. They'd been told it would 'instantly disable any attacker.' They were cocky. One even said, 'We're going to wipe you guys up.' The experiment was arranged to give them many more advantages than they'd have in a real assault—the tear gas was in their hands, not in their purses, and they knew they'd be using it. After the test, they were all very upset. They felt they'd been misled by the tear gas school."

"We were as surprised as the women were," coproducer Karen Winters recalls. "We believed the tear gas school's promotional videotape. It showed assailants instantly incapacitated."

Even with the tear gas in hand, the women hit the deputies "no more than 20 percent of the time," Giles explains. "They hit them in the face even less." In the few cases where the officers were hit in the face, "the spray did not stop them. The manufacturers' claim of 'immediate incapacitation' simply did not hold true. Those deputies hit in the face did feel some ill effects, but only after a minute or so, which wouldn't stop a real assault."

Nonetheless, there have been many reports of people using tear gas successfully against attackers. There have also been reports of assailants turning it against those attempting to defend themselves, or using it as an offensive weapon. If the VCSD/"20/20" tests showed tear gas to be completely ineffective, how can these reports be explained?

Lieutenant Giles says tear gas effectiveness depends on two things: surprise and pain. An assailant may be deterred not by the chemical, but by the surprise when the intended target resists the victim role by brandishing it. In other words, tear gas might break the holding mechanism during the confrontation stage. In addition, different people have different tolerances for pain. Assuming good aim, the chemical might take effect fast enough against some people but Giles warns, "Don't bet on it. In my opinion, the claims made for tear gas are baloney."

Like a pistol, tear gas may also engender a false sense of security. You think you're protected but are you? "People are certainly free to carry it," Giles says, "but I don't recommend it. It's no substitute for staying alert on the street."

• *Shriek Alarms, Police Whistles, and Skunk Bomb.* A shriek alarm is a pocket-size canister that emits a truly ear-splitting whine when triggered. A "nonweapon," it cannot physically harm an attacker (though if discharged into a telephone against an obscene caller, it may cause hearing impairment). By the same token, it cannot be turned against you. Shriek alarms and police whistles work by breaking the holding mechanism during the confrontation stage. They let potential assailants know that you are a resister and that any attempted assault may not go according to plan. Shriek alarms are impossible to ignore, especially at close range. They will startle anyone and may well give you the split second necessary to escape. They may also attract others. In fact, in some communities people have organized "whistle brigades." Members carry the same type of noisemaker, recognize its sound, and respond if they hear it. Because they are nonweapons, however, noise-making devices tend not to engender any false sense of security. Shriek alarms are sold in drug and variety stores, or by mail.

Rapel Rape deterrent is another useful nonweapon. The name is misleading; it's appropriate not only against rapists, but against any street attacker. Rapel is a small vial of synthetic skunk odor that deters assailants by disgusting them. The vial may be hand-held or clipped to clothing. It can be triggered with one hand, which helps if you're caught by surprise. Once activated, it releases a truly noxious stench that pervades the immediate vicinity. The manufacturer says it will send any assailant fleeing. After testing it, I tend to agree. The smell is horrible. The odor clings to the attacker and marks him, which may help in apprehension. It also clings to you, but Rapel provides a neutralizer to remove it. Like shriek alarms, Rapel cannot be turned against you, and it's unlikely to engender a false sense of security. Rapel may not stop every assailant every time, but it carries Nature's own seal of approval—it's worked quite well for the skunk.

• *Umbrellas, Canes, and Walking Sticks.* Concealed weapons, whether they're guns, knives, or skunk bomb, all share one significant disadvantage—an assailant sizing you up cannot see them. You may be able to use them to defend yourself during the confrontation or altercation stages of an assault, but the best deterrents are the earliest, those that dissuade during the invitation stage, for example, nonvictim movement and traveling in groups. In addition to these precautions, however, you might consider carrying an umbrella, cane, or walking stick. Their main advantage is visibility from a distance. A visible implement, combined with a sprightly step that shows you don't need it to help you walk, may well persuade an assailant that you're not an attractive target.

ASSAULT PREVENTION FOR THE DISABLED

Among the most vulnerable-looking targets for muggers and rapists are the disabled. But disabilities need not condemn anyone to
criminal victimization. Quite the contary, according to Laurie Ann
Lepoff, a brown belt in jujitsu, who teaches self-defense to disabled
people in Berkeley, California.

"It doesn't matter if you're able-bodied or disabled," Lepoff says.
"The basics of street safety are the same: Pay close attention to
what's going on around you and don't hesitate to act on your intuition. Then go out accompanied if possible, stay in lighted, well-trav-
eled areas, and if you're attacked and choose to resist, fight furiously
and fight dirty."

Although disabled people may look vulnerable, Lepoff says they
generally have one crucial self-defense advantage, the element of surprise. "The average mugger is less guarded when attacking a disabled
person. He's certainly not brave. What kind of person assaults someone who's disabled? He doesn't imagine there will be any resistance.
When there is, he's usually quite surprised. In my classes I teach disabled people to take full advantage of that surprise. Often, at the first
sign that the person does not intend to be a victim, the assailant calls
off the attack."

Lepoff also teaches her students to decide when weapons would be
appropriate—not guns, knives, or tear gas, none of which she recommends—but unconventional weapons that preserve the element of
surprise, for example, pencils or hatpins. "What mugger expects
somebody in a wheelchair to stab him with a sharp pencil?" But Lepoff adds that she never recommends using any weapon without
training and a good deal of practice.

Have any of her disabled students successfully defended themselves against street assaults? Lepoff replies, "You bet they have."

STREET VIOLENCE CAN BE
REDUCED 50 PERCENT

The life-style adjustments required to prevent most assaults are relatively minor and based largely on foresight and common sense. Violent street crimes cannot be entirely prevented, but authorities estimate they could be reduced at least 50 percent and assaults that did occur would cause fewer injuries and deaths.

Since my mugging ten years ago, I've often wondered how I would react to another street confrontation. As I finished work on this book, I had an opportunity to find out. I returned home one night at about 11 P.M. and parked a block from my door in a medium-assault-risk neighborhood of San Francisco. As I walked home, I noticed four young men walking abreast up the sidewalk toward me. They were about twenty yards away.

I stopped and focused on them. It was too dark to see their faces, but they looked about sixteen or seventeen. Three seemed about my size, but one was bigger. As soon as they saw me their pace slowed and they split into two groups of two. One pair took the street side of the sidewalk, the other, the building side, leaving me no alternative but to walk between them if I continued on my way. Then the big one took his hands out of his pockets. They were fifteen yards away.

Almost without thinking, I crossed the street. I was tired, but I set myself—balanced and centered. I moved quickly, my arms swinging, both eyes on them, and thought, No way, guys, you won't even get close.

I headed for the opposite corner, then stood there poised to move in any direction, and watched them saunter up the street. When they passed directly across from me, the big one turned my way and shouted, "Hey, man, smart move!"

I couldn't believe he actually said that, but he did. I made no reply, but kept watching as they continued on their way. Would they have attacked me or were they just a bunch of loud-mouthed kids trying to act tough? I'll never know. But I'm glad I didn't have to find out the hard way.

Resources:

The I.C.A. Method of Self-Protection
Joel Kirsch, Ph.D.
P.O. Box 258
Mill Valley, CA 94941

Kirsch teaches one- and two-day assault-prevention workshops as a consultant to corporations and community groups.

Tenderloin Senior Escort Program
Glide Memorial United Methodist Church
330 Ellis St., Suite 608
San Francisco, CA 94102

The Sound Alarm
(a shriek alarm)
For price and shipping information, write:
Sound Alarm Co.
1312 Washington Ave.
St. Louis, MO 63103

Rapel Rape Deterrent
$10.00
Rapel Products
P.O. Box 15227
Austin, TX 78761

If you use it, send the manufacturer a copy of the police report, and get a replacement vial free.

"Crime Prevention Program" (8th revision)
95 pages; price information from:
George Sunderland, Crime Prevention Program Coordinator
National Retired Teachers Association/
American Association of Retired Persons
1909 K St. N.W.
Washington, DC 20049
(202) 872–4700

A good introduction to assault prevention for older people.

5

How to Prevent Burglary . . . and What to Do if You Can't

WELCOME TO THE BIG CITY

One Sunday afternoon nine years ago, my wife and I went to the beach to take a break from setting up a new apartment. We were gone no more than two hours. When we returned the front door was slightly ajar. I knew I'd locked it on the way out; I've always been a stickler about locking doors. Fearing the worst, I yelled, "We're home!" to give anyone inside a chance to leave through the back door. But the apartment was silent. And cleaned out.

We'd just moved from a suburb in Michigan to San Francisco. We didn't have that much; everything fit into a U-Haul trailer. But the burglars (I've always felt there were more than one) took every valuable we had: the TV, stereo, jewelry, electric typewriter, and my new leather briefcase. Welcome to the Big City.

First we called the police, then surveyed the scene. They had broken in through a rear window off the back stairs. The window was wide open with fingerprints on the sill. I knew I'd locked it, but its old, double-hung sashes did not fit snugly, and the lock, a common clamshell clasp, must have been jimmied with a knife wedged up between the sashes.

It seemed probable—indeed, almost certain—that the burglars

either lived in the immediate vicinity or were assisted by someone who did. We had been gone only a short time. The window opened into a private alley accessible only to other apartments in our building. Its street access was secured by a locked metal gate. The only other access was over a high fence that led to a private alley for the building next door.

We alerted a neighbor (all the while wondering if *he* was the one). He shook his head in apparently sincere disgust and said there had been a rash of break-ins around the neighborhood. He'd lived in the building for several years and had a good feel for the area. He suspected some people across the street. They'd lived in our building the previous year and were "weird." They still might have a key to the alley door. . . .

I suppressed my rage by focusing on how I'd assist the police in catching the burglars and recovering our property. The police lab could lift the fingerprints and begin the identification process, while the city's finest and I visited the half-dozen neighbors who could have been involved to see if they had our things. I felt certain we'd find something I could identify. We'd recover our property, and the police would close the case in less time than it took to watch a Sherlock Holmes movie. Not quite.

Two officers arrived an hour after we called. The younger one offered condolences. His partner simply shrugged and began filling out the case report.

When I showed them the fingerprints and mentioned the lab, they replied, "We never call the lab for burglaries. Just serious crimes." Well, what was this, *a prank?* I pointed out my neighbor-involvement theory, and the suspicions surrounding the people across the street, but when I suggested that we knock on a few doors, their eyes glazed over. "We never do that for burglaries." How about the detectives? Don't *they* investigate burglaries? "Almost never. Just serious crimes."

I was furious, angrier at the police than at the burglars. The officers completed their report and explained how to obtain a copy for our insurance company. When they left, I felt we'd been ripped off twice in three hours.

In a daze, I wandered from room to newly emptied room. They'd taken everything except $200 in cash stashed in a book on a low shelf in the study. At first, I felt worst about losing my briefcase because it was custom-made and could not be replaced. But in the days that followed, the typewriter, the tool of my trade, weighed heaviest.

There was a locksmith around the corner. I bought two of everything. I secured the apartment so tightly that my wife objected, and we wound up not using several of the locks I installed.

Gradually, anger gave way to the pain of loss. I replaced my dear departed Smith-Corona and slowly our lives returned to normal. A few months later, the insurance settlement arrived—case closed, except that ever since I check the doors and windows *twice* before going anywhere. Otherwise, I hardly think about it unless I see someone carrying a distinctive leather briefcase. I still wonder who's carrying mine. . . .

ANATOMY OF THE TYPICAL BURGLARY

In more ways than I imagined at the time, our burglary was typical. It happened in a city, in a high-risk area for burglary. We were renters in our midtwenties and we'd just moved in. We were prime targets.

Our burglary also happened in the afternoon. The stereotype is that burglary is a nighttime crime, and most people leave lights on when they're away after dark to make the house look occupied. But *more than half* of all burglaries occur during the day. Ray Thomson, a Philadelphia police burglary specialist, says, "At one time we thought burglars worked almost exclusively at night, but not anymore. The typical burglary occurs between noon and three P.M." To be sure, many burglaries still occur at night (about 40 percent), but the trend is clearly toward daytime break-ins. From 1976 through 1980, the rate of daytime burglaries increased three times faster than nighttime break-ins. Why? Largely because more people than ever live in one-person households, and almost half of all women now work outside the home. As a result, the typical dwelling is more likely to be unoccupied during the day than at night.

Our burglary appeared to have been committed by people who lived nearby. That's the rule. An in-depth Justice Department study showed that two-thirds of the "most typical" group of burglars (men under eighteen) traveled less than a mile from home to commit their crimes. Many police say burglars work even closer to their base. Ray Thomson says the typical burglar "lives within three blocks of the homes he burglarizes."

We were thankful to be spared physical confrontation with our intruders. Burglars prefer it that way, too. Residents confront them in no more than 10 percent of break-ins.

Our burglars did not ransack the apartment. They took what they could carry easily and unload quickly. The estimates vary, but authorities generally agree that most residential burglars are in and out in five minutes. Ex-burglar Marcus Ratledge writes that he and the many B&E men he knew in prison rarely spent more than five minutes inside the homes they plundered. They take the TV and the stereo. They check desk drawers, the silverware cabinet, the family room, and any work areas. If they ransack anything, they usually concentrate on bedroom closets, dresser drawers and nightstands, grabbing any jewelry, cash, and firearms they find. Then they leave. They tend to miss valuables hidden with even minimal creativity; as they did with our $200 hidden in a book. Security equipment makers may spur sales with tales of master thieves who take homes apart nail by nail, but the vast majority of burglaries are quick once-over affairs.

Finally, our burglary typified police—especially urban police—reactions to crimes that do not involve violence. They treated our burglary as routine, even boring. Our loss wasn't "serious enough" to call the lab or a detective. At the time, I felt they were shirking their duty, but the fact is, they did all they could. During the research for this book, I discussed those officers' reactions with many police. They all said, "You watch too much television." TV cops may call the lab, but in reality, this happens only for violent crimes, and even then, the results are rarely impressive. TV detectives never miss, but real detectives make arrests in *less than 5 percent* of their cases. Those arrests are made the way most are, not as a result of investigative finesse, but because the burglar finally slipped up, or an alarm sounded, or an observant neighbor got a license number, or recognized some neighborhood kids as the perpetrators. Burglaries are reported to police around the country once every eight seconds, far too often to mobilize concerted reactions, especially when violent crimes are (and should be) the priority. In Charles Silberman's words: "We expect more than the police can deliver. We need to lower our expectations. [Once a crime has been committed] there is little the police can do."

This judgment, shared by many police, raises serious questions about traditional reactive police work, but with regard to crime prevention, it's no cause for despair. Recall that most criminals are young, green and scared. One reason they burglarize is the low risk of confrontation with victims. The hallmark of burglary is not skill, but opportunity. Remove the opportunity and in most cases, you deter the crime. *The bottom line is that the average person is much better equipped to prevent burglary than the average burglar is to commit it.*

The rest of this and the following chapter list proven ways to prevent home and auto burglary, bicycle and auto theft, rural crime, and fraud. In an effort to be comprehensive, I've risked implying that you're a sitting duck unless you take every precaution. This is *not* the case. These recommendations offer a smorgasbord of alternatives to choose from. The emphasis is on those that are simple, cost-effective, and relatively nondisruptive of daily life. Start with the one or two that help you feel safer right now. You can always take additional precautions as your personal crime-prevention program progresses.

FIRST-LINE DEFENSES: REMEMBER 7-ELEVEN

There are three lines of defense against burglary. First-line defenses deter burglars from approaching your home, and if they do, from walking in without effort. Second-line precautions prevent them from breaking in. Third-line defenses deter all but the most skilled, determined, or reckless.

Recall that the 7-Eleven robbery-prevention program increases the visibility of store interiors by moving registers and window advertising, and installing outside lights to make robbers feel that they are on stage. This approach also works against burglars, who are even more visibility-shy than robbers.

• *Trim trees and bushes to increase visibility of doors and windows.* Lower fences that block views of front or back doors. In one study where convicted burglars were taken to residential neighborhoods to point out attractive targets, they consistently selected homes with fences, hedges, or large shrubs that blocked visibility and offered concealment (see figure 5–1).

• *Install outside lighting.* In the study just mentioned, the burglars also preferred homes with poor outside lighting and no nearby street lights. Floodlights are not necessary; forty-watt bulbs near doors and along walkways should suffice. Timers set from dusk to dawn are also a good idea, especially for those who regularly return home after dark.

• *Consider ornamental plants with spines.* Rose bushes, holly, or cacti help deter burglary.

• *Eliminate concealed vestibules.* Either open them up by trimming shrubbery and installing lighting, or close them off with secure doors, locks, and window grilles.

• *Warning stickers.* The 7-Eleven program uses perimeter stickers to put robbers "on notice" that clerks cannot open the safe. Operation Identification, a fundamental part of police-sponsored crime-prevention programs, uses the same principle. Police lend residents engraving tools to mark valuables with identification numbers. The theory is that "branded" property is difficult for burglars to sell. However, an Illinois study showed that "identification markings (alone) did not significantly reduce opportunities to dispose of stolen property, or increase its recovery," and interviews with Illinois burglars showed that they were not reluctant to steal marked valuables. Nonetheless, burglary rates among Operation Identification participants consistently decline. Why? Because participants also target-harden their homes.

The *real* value of Operation Identification has less to do with property marking than with the perimeter stickers police provide: "Warning! All articles have been marked and recorded with the Police Department." The stickers put burglars on notice that the residents are security conscious. Although property marking by itself has little effect, in the context of other precautions, Operation ID homes are less attractive targets.

LOCK UP: REDUCE RISK UP TO 40 PERCENT

• *Lock doors and windows when you're home as well as when you're out.* A Justice Department study of residential burglaries

Figure 5-1: First-line Burglary Defenses: 1. Outside lighting 2. Foundation shrubbery trimmed 3. Rose bushes 4. Operation Identification stickers 5. "Beware of Dog" sign 6. In-door mail slot 7. Lights and radio on

93

shows that a staggering *44 percent* do not involve break-ins at all, but *let-ins* through unlocked doors, open windows, or keys left under doormats. An unlocked door is an open invitation. It's so easy to lock up. It takes no time, no investment in security hardware, and it largely prevents crimes by neighborhood boys, who might otherwise find it difficult to pass up an easy opportunity. When locking up, don't forget the garage. Many garden tools can be used as burglary tools, and many break-ins—and rapes—occur when a ladder is used to gain entry through an open second-story window.

• *Don't leave keys under doormats.* Even the greenest twelve-year-old will look there. If you hide a house key, hide it several steps from the door.

• *Leave lights on to make your home look occupied.* Leaving lights on—or better yet a radio or television—might persuade a burglar casing the area to move on. The enthusiasm for illuminating empty homes has worked wonders for sales of light timers; from simple, single-light devices ($10), to photosensitive timers that turn lights on at sunset and off at dawn ($30 to $50), to multiple-input "home controllers" that can turn many lights and appliances on and off at different times ($50 to $200). Light timers are a reasonable investment, but before you spend a lot of money, remember: most burglaries occur *during the day,* when lights are off, and even with the best timer, a simple knock on the door is all it takes to determine whether anyone is home.

• *Valuables should not be visible from the street.* Especially portable valuables: TVs, stereos, cameras, and firearms; they're magnets for burglars.

• *Consider replacing a mailbox with an in-door mail slot.* Visible mail signals vacancy.

• *Consider getting a dog.* Dogs require care, but if you enjoy them as pets, large, loud, territorial dogs can provide burglary protection, *if* they're in the house when intruders attempt to enter. If you have a dog, "Beware of Dog" signs are a good idea, no matter what the dog's temperament. For referrals to watchdog training classes, call your local humane society.

• *Consider "watch geese."* Adult geese are extremely territorial, and make good guard animals for some people. When stationed in an enclosed yard, the twenty-pound birds behave like pets around people they recognize, but charge others while flapping their large, powerful wings, honking and screaming. They make more noise than many dogs, and rarely fail to startle intruders and signal neighbors. On the downside, however, geese cannot be housebroken. They are not as smart as dogs and may eat newspapers, mail, and ornamental plants.

• *Announce weddings and funerals cautiously.* Ray Johnson promotes the 7-Eleven program through the media because "crooks read newspapers as much as anyone else." Apparently they pay special attention to wedding and funeral announcements, which broadcast when certain households are likely to be unoccupied or preoccupied. Weddings and funerals also attract visitors and cars unfamiliar to neighbors, thus reducing a burglar's risk of being singled out. The commotion of family occasions provides good cover for theft (or casing), and at weddings, a selection of gifts to steal. Finally, neighbors often attend these functions, reducing the likelihood that intruders will be noticed. It's not prudent to publicize family events in advance. Friends and relatives can be enlisted to spread the word to those who should know. For others, post-event announcements should suffice.

SECOND-LINE DEFENSES:
FREE SECURITY SURVEYS

Almost any lock—if locked—deters neighborhood kids from walking off with your television. But to stop burglars who actually *break* in, hardware considerations become crucial. Second-line defenses, called "target-hardening" by crime-prevention experts, make the biggest difference in reducing the risk of break-ins. In Portland, Oregon, a police-sponsored target-hardening program for senior citizens cut burglaries an astonishing 88 percent in one year. A similar program in Seattle cut burglaries in four public housing projects 60 percent, and the crime-prevention data base at the National Criminal Justice Reference Service in Rockville, Maryland, is filled with similar success stories.

Effective home security requires an understanding of how burglars actually gain entry. About 80 percent get in through doors, 20 percent through windows.

The best way to begin securing your home is to consult someone who can recommend hardware appropriate to your specific needs. Before you rush off and spend a fortune on steel doors, "pickproof" locks, and window grilles, call your local police crime-prevention unit. Most provide security surveys *for free*. Even if you think you live in a fortress, a security survey is well worth it. One New Yorker, who felt safe behind his massive front door and locked windows, found the experience "impressive and disturbing":

The officer walked straight to the essential openings. He stared at the fire escape. What's at the bottom of it? Where does the air shaft go? How far is it to the next building? He recommended folding gates for the windows that opened onto the fire escape and a new lock for the fire-escape door. He shook his head over the front door: "It wouldn't stand up to serious attack." He crisply detailed the inadequacies of the hinges, the jambs, and the lock. He drew diagrams, gave ball-park prices for hardware, and later hand-delivered a written report. Makes you think.

HARDWARE: REDUCE RISK UP TO 85 PERCENT

My brother David says many people waste a fortune on security hardware. He ought to know. He's a locksmith and he's secured thousands of homes. One of his favorite "wasted money" stories concerns an apartment he was once called in to secure after it had been burglarized. The owner had installed everything: a solid-core door, a heavy-duty dead bolt with a pick-resistant cylinder, a chain lock, a peephole, and a "police" lock with a steel bar that secured the door to the floor. The door frame was reinforced with metal strips. How had the burglar gotten in? He sledge-hammered a hole through the plasterboard wall next to the door frame, then reached inside and unlocked all the hardware. The break-in probably took less than a minute. Instead of that door's $500 worth of hardware, a simple double-cylinder dead bolt (key operated inside and out) would have prevented entry. (This burglar must have known that the apartment did not have a double-cylinder lock; burglars almost never go through walls.) The point is, home security can be tricky. Unless you really know what you're doing, hire a locksmith to install appropriate hardware.

Locksmiths can be expensive. Depending on the condition of your doors and frames, locksmithing might cost $60 to $300 for each exterior door. Of course, cost should be weighed against benefit. Locksmithing is a one-time expense, unlike property insurance, which can cost that much every year. In 1980, the average burglary loss was $882, and that says nothing about the emotional trauma involved. But if you'd rather do it yourself, these two books are excellent: *The Complete Book of Locks, Keys, Burglar and Smoke Alarms, and Other Security Devices*, by Eugene A. Sloane; and *Home Security*, edited by William Frankell.

Here's the advice locksmiths offer on cost-effective target-hardening:

• *Solid-core doors front and back.* A lock is only as good as the door it's mounted on. Never use hollow doors for entrances or for inside doors you need secured. In most areas, solid wood doors (1-3/4 inches thick) should suffice. In high-risk areas, metal doors might be more appropriate, or wood doors reinforced with sheet metal (see figure 5–2).

• *Solid door jambs front and back.* A door is only as good as the frame it fits into. In most "crowbar jobs," it's the frame that gets damaged, not the door. The door should close flush against the jamb, and the entire frame should be as solid as the door. Steel strips can be used to reinforce door frames in high-risk areas.

• *Hinges on the inside.* This prevents hinge removal, then subsequent door removal. If hinges must be mounted on the outside, they should be secured. The easiest, least expensive way is to remove a facing pair of hinge screws, one from the door, one from the jamb. Then hammer a twenty-penny nail into the door-jamb hole, leaving a half-inch of the nail exposed, and cut off the nail head with a hacksaw. When you close the door, the exposed metal pin should fit into the opposite screw hole and secure the door even if the hinge pin is removed.

• *Minimize glass in doors.* The less glass, the better. If you like windows in doors for aesthetic reasons, consider replacing glass with clear plastic. Two kinds are available, acrylic plastic (Plexiglas) and polycarbonate resin (Lexan). Acrylic plastic generally stops a thrown brick, but breaks if attacked with a hammer or crowbar. It's recommended for garages and sheds where the major risk is vandalism, not burglary (unless the outbuilding holds a ladder, in which case bur-

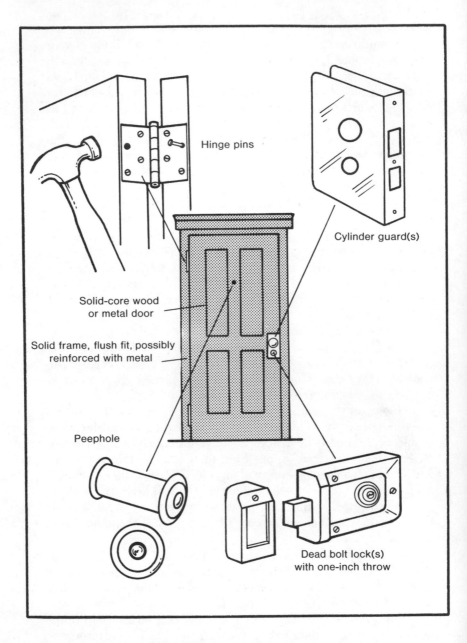

FIGURE 5-2: Door Security

glary risk should be considered). Polycarbonate resin is almost indestructible; it can withstand sledgehammer blows. The only way to get past it is to remove it, which involves more time and effort than most burglars are willing to invest. Another approach is to install double-cylinder dead bolts—see page 101.

• *Use a peephole to inspect visitors, not a chain lock.* Chain locks are simply not reliable. They can be broken with a strong blow or cut with bolt cutters. Inspect your visitors from behind a securely locked door. The simplest way is to install a wide-angle peephole. Peepholes are inexpensive (about $5) and easy to mount. Just drill a hole through the door and screw the two halves of the peephole into each other.

• *Never rely on key-in-knob locks.* Knob locks, popular with builders because they're inexpensive, are a magnet for burglars. Many can be defeated with a knife or credit card jammed between the door and the frame. The rest can be removed with a hammer or crowbar. The burglar simply breaks off the knob, and with it, the lock.

• *Never rely on slip bolt locks.* Slip locks, also known as night latches or slam locks, have spring-loaded, beveled bolts. If the tapered side of the bolt faces out, the usual arrangement, the lock may be opened with a knife or credit card. Even if the angled side faces in, you are still in jeopardy; the spring that holds the bolt is rarely strong enough to resist determined attack (see figure 5–3).

• *Use dead bolt locks on all entry doors.* Dead bolts (and rim locks—see page 101) are the best security investment for the average door. The bolt is neither beveled nor spring-loaded. It must be advanced and retracted manually, with a thumb wheel or key. Depending on the model, the bolt advances either a half-inch or an inch. Locksmiths recommend the latter ("one-inch throw").

Dead bolts are best, but they are neither indestructible nor pick-proof. They don't have to be. No lock is ever absolutely tamperproof. For home security, the criterion of effectiveness is not impenetrability, but rather the ability to withstand attack (by crowbar, vice grips, or drill) for five minutes. If a burglar cannot break in with a minimum of noise and struggle in three or four minutes, he'll move on.

What about lock picking? Given enough time, concentration, and perseverance, locksmiths can usually pick open even "pick-resistant"

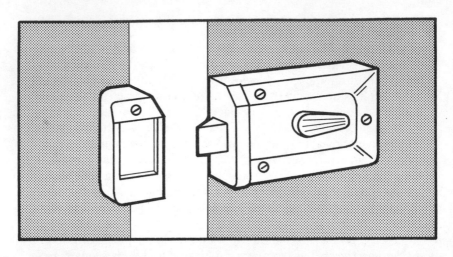

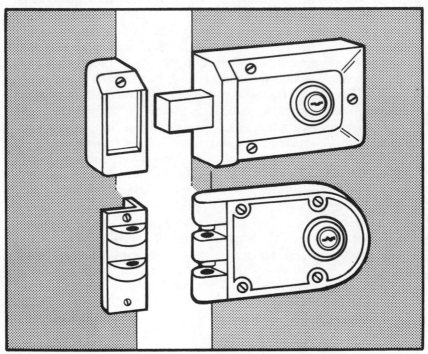

Figure 5–3: Slip Locks *vs.* Dead Bolt Locks

100

locks, but residential and small-business burglars rarely, if ever, have the skills to do this. Ex-burglar Marcus Ratledge writes: "Television and movies [imply that] burglars can pick any lock or wire any alarm system. I assure you, only one burglar in 10,000 is this accomplished." Ratledge reconfirms what we already know about street criminals: They are overwhelmingly unskilled opportunists with short attention spans. If you delay them just a few minutes, they leave.

Consumer Reports tested dead bolts and concluded that three showed "excellent resistance to assault" on the condition that the bolt advanced into a metal jamb or a high-security strike plate (see page 102). The three were: Medeco Ultra 700, Medeco D11200, and Schlage B560P.

Among dead bolts, double-cylinder models, which require key opening on both sides of the door, provide the best security. They prevent a burglar who gets in through a window from carrying your stereo out a door. Forcing the burglar to exit the way he entered slows him down, reduces losses, and attracts neighbors' attention. A man walking out your front door with a TV could be a friend borrowing it, but the same man climbing out a window would automatically arouse suspicion.

Double-cylinder locks, however, have certain disadvantages. If you surprise a burglar in your home (unlikely but possible), they can hinder his escape and may force a confrontation, with the possibility of serious injury. They are also a fire evacuation hazard, particularly if there are small children, elderly, or disabled people in the home. To deal with this, some people leave a key in the inside cylinder when they're home. Locksmiths discourage this. You might slip into the habit of leaving it there all the time, which would defeat the purpose. Also, the inside key might interfere with outside key operation, and lock you out. A better approach is to leave a key close by—but hidden so an intruder could not let himself out.

In high-risk areas, security experts generally recommend *two* dead bolts per exterior door to spread the impact of any heavy blows. For secondary dead bolts, rim locks are usually sufficient (see below).

• *Rim locks.* Also called "drop bolts" or "vertical dead bolts," the bolts on rim locks advance into a set of heavy metal rings. Single- and double-cylinder models are available. *Consumer Reports* rated "very good": Ideal Super Guard Lock I DB9285, and Sears Catalogue no. 58461.

• *Proper lock installation is crucial.* Locks should be mounted to prevent removal without considerable time, noise, and struggle. Good dead bolts come with one-way ("allen") screws that secure them in place. Lock bolts should not advance only into the wood of the door jamb, but also into a metal jamb or "strike plate" secured by long screws. In high-risk areas, larger "super strike plates" provide extra protection by spreading the impact of any blows.

• *Protect your protection.* It's best to cover exterior door locks with metal cylinder guards, which prevent the locks from being pried out of the door by leaving access only to the keyhole. Cylinder guards cost about $5 each, and advertise that the residents understand security.

• *Special locks.* Most locksmiths would say that homes neither in high-risk areas nor filled with unusually valuable items can be adequately secured with good dead bolts professionally installed in well-mounted, solid-core doors, with peepholes and a minimum of glass. But some situations may require added protection, and some people may desire extra hardware. A "buttress lock," also called a "police" or "barricade" lock (around $100 installed) uses a steel bar to lock the door to a socket on the floor a few feet away. The bar braces the door. Buttress locks, however, are no substitute for solid-core (or metal) doors. A "crossbar lock" ($150 to $200 installed) sends two horizontal steel bars into sockets in the door jambs. A "spider" or "mul-T-lock" ($225 to $300 installed) is a variation on the crossbar; it uses four steel bolts instead of two: one above the door, one below, and one in each jamb. Special locks provide added security but tend to look unsightly.

• *If your new home already has dead bolt locks, change the key combinations.* Periodic changes are also a good idea if you lend keys, then lose track of them.

• *Sliding glass doors.* Sliding doors are as popular with burglars as they are with homeowners. The locks built into them offer no security and should *never* be relied on. Securing sliding glass doors effectively involves two steps: locking the sliding panel, and preventing it from being lifted out of its track. The simplest and least expensive way to lock a sliding door is to place a broom handle in the floor track. Another is to mount a pivoting barricade bar ("charley bar") in the middle of the stationary panel. It serves the same purpose as a broom handle, but is more visible from a distance, and advertises residents' security consciousness. A third approach is to use dead bolts designed for sliding doors. They can lock the door closed, or open a few inches for ventilation. They also prevent it from being lifted out of its track. If you decide to use a broom handle instead of a dead bolt, the cheapest way to secure the door in its track is to drill holes at ten-inch intervals in the upper track. Then drive 1-1/2-inch sheet metal screws into each hole, allowing the heads to protrude enough to prevent the door from being removed while still allowing it to slide normally (see figure 5-4).

• *Windows.* Windows are obviously more difficult to secure than doors because glass is easy to break. Plastic glass substitutes have already been mentioned. Metal grilles are another option. Recall that 20 percent of burglars gain entry through windows, but relatively few break glass. It's noisy and attracts attention (except in some rural areas).

• *Fit all wood-sash windows with "vent locks."* The standard wood-sash window lock, the clamshell clasp that locks the sashes together, has two serious drawbacks: it provides no security when the window is open, and it may be jimmied with a knife forced up between them. Vent locks solve both these problems. They secure the window when it's open, and they cannot be jimmied. The simplest vent lock requires only two nails per window (see figure 5-5). With the window closed, drill holes in both upper corners of the lower sash that extend into the lower corners of the upper sash. Angle the holes slightly downward. Nails inserted in the holes lock the window closed. Then raise the window about three inches and repeat the process. The nails may now be used to lock it open. Don't open the window too far in the open-locked position; even if an adult can't get in, a child might be able to. Some burglars boost small children into partly open windows, then the kids open the window farther, or open a door. Commercial vent locks come in several models, either with or without keys. (Keyed vent locks may present a fire evacuation hazard.) Vent locks are as important on second-story windows as on ground-floor windows. The "second-story man" who specializes in upper floor entries is a myth. Burglars don't specialize, but with the assistance of the resident's ladder (or a neighbor's), second-story entry might be the path of least resistance.

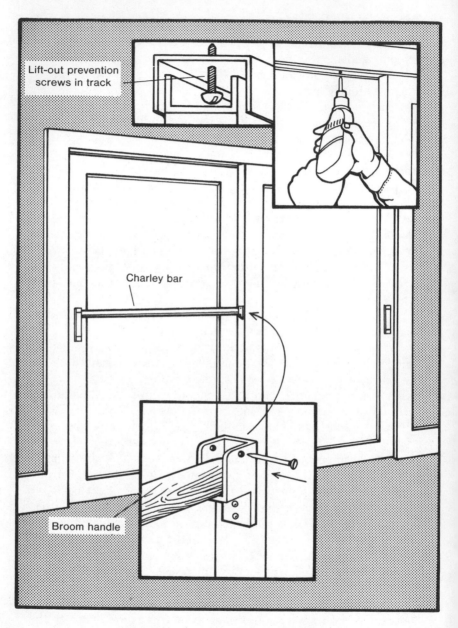

Lift-out prevention screws in track

Charley bar

Broom handle

Figure 5–4: Sliding Door Security

104

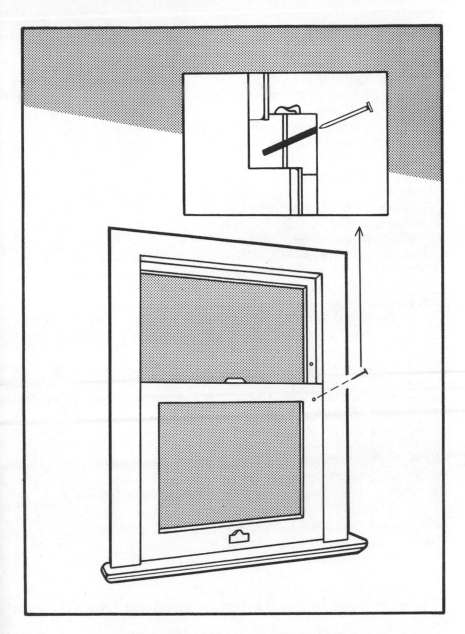

Figure 5–5: Do-It-Yourself Vent Locks

105

• *Metal-frame windows.* Sliding metal windows can be secured like sliding glass doors. For crank-operated windows, either remove the crank to a place more than an arm's length away, or install locks (consider fire evacuation hazard). Don't forget to secure skylights.

• *Basement windows.* If basement windows are never opened, nail them shut. If they are used, or if you want to preserve them as fire exits, install vent locks. Basement windows may be too small for adults, but not for children.

• *Consider grillework for high-risk windows and doors.* Few precautions advertise residents' understanding of security more than metal grilles. Grillework can be expensive, but if you live in a high-risk area, it might be worth it. For some windows, a full grille might not be necessary; a simple S-shaped piece of metal might suffice. Some people do not like the feeling of living behind bars. The look of grillework may be softened by selecting a more decorative, less barlike style, or by planting vines that turn grilles into trellises. Keep fire evacuation in mind. Doors and windows that might be used as fire exits should be fitted with "break-away" grilles that can be opened from the inside. Wire mesh prevents them from being opened from the outside (see figure 5–6).

• *Secure window-mounted air conditioners.* Make sure they cannot be easily removed, and that windows lock around them.

• *Lock garages and sheds.* Garage doors are best secured with dead bolts, rim locks, or padlocks. When choosing a padlock, look for:

• a laminated steel case to resist smashing
• a thick (9/32") case-hardened steel shackle with the word "hardened" stamped on
• a "double-locking shackle," both ends mechanically secured inside the case
• a precision locking mechanism
• corrosion protection against the elements
• a hasp that leaves no screws exposed when locked

THIRD-LINE DEFENSES: ARE ALARMS NECESSARY?

Burglar alarms are the icing on the home-security cake. Most burglars prefer to avoid them. A study in Portland, Oregon, showed that

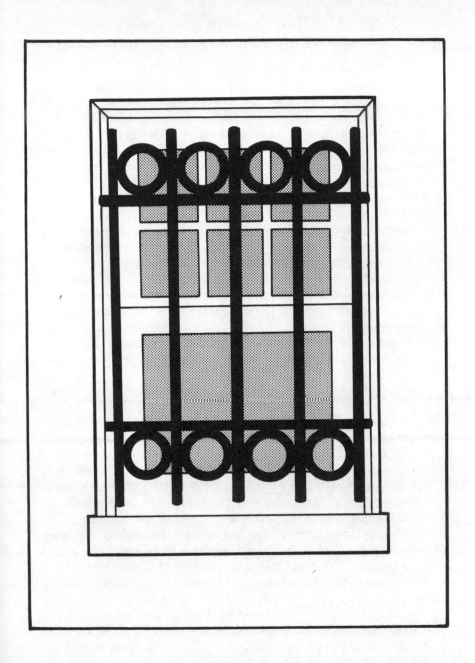

Figure 5–6: Window Grillework

107

homes without alarms were *six times* more likely to be burglarized than homes with them. Another study in Cedar Rapids, Iowa, identified matched pairs of businesses and schools, then wired one of each with an alarm system centrally monitored by local police. Attempted burglaries were 41 percent lower at the alarm-wired businesses, 50 percent lower at the schools. In addition, arrests at the scene occurred in 31 percent of burglaries at wired sites, but in only 6 percent of burglaries at locations without them. These statistics are impressive, but the case for investing in an alarm is by no means open and shut.

Alarm systems have three basic components: sensors that detect intrusion; an alarm mechanism; and a power supply. Sensors come in many forms: magnetic contacts, pressure mats, electric eyes, ultrasonic devices, and microwave motion detectors.

There are three kinds of alarm mechanisms: on-site bells; so-called "silent" alarms that ring at police stations, or more typically, at alarm company facilities; and combinations of the two. Alarm options are now available in some cable television packages, and monitoring functions have been incorporated into some home computer programs.

The typical system uses the home's regular power supply, with a backup battery in case of blackout (or wire-cutting by burglars). In good on-site bell systems, the alarm rings for fifteen minutes, then shuts off and resets automatically.

The cost of the many alarm alternatives varies considerably. *Consumer Reports* rated twenty-three relatively inexpensive, off-the-shelf systems in the $100 to $700 range, but warned: "These systems wouldn't be much challenge to seasoned thieves. A professionally installed system might be a better investment if you have unusually valuable things to protect." Not surprisingly, professional alarm installers scoff at install-it-yourself systems. They say homeowners would do better to spend the money it takes to buy an off-the-shelf system on top-quality locks instead. Install-it-yourself alarm systems may deter some burglars, but there is no research to demonstrate this. The only alarms with proven effectiveness are professionally installed systems monitored by central stations, which usually cost $750 to $2,000, plus about $250 a year for monitoring services. (Some homeowners insurance policies offer discounts for homes with centrally monitored systems.)

The National Burglar and Fire Alarm Association reports that Americans spend $110 million a year on burglar alarms. But despite the widely publicized increased fear of crime (fear grimly celebrated in alarm advertising), *no more than 3 percent* of American homes (and 20 percent of businesses) have alarm systems. Before you invest, consider:

• *Response time.* The mere presence of a good system, advertised with entry-point stickers, will scare off many burglars, but an important part of the motivation for investing in an alarm is the idea that police will respond promptly to any calls. Rapid response is a major reason alarm experts recommend combination systems. The bell puts the burglar on notice that he's been detected and may move a neighbor to call the police. But even if neighbors do not respond as soon as the alarm sounds, either the police or alarm company personnel swing into action—at least in theory. Generally, the wealthier the community, the faster the response. But what about response time in *your* community? Before you invest in an alarm system, investigate the experiences of alarm owners in your immediate vicinity. Response times of twenty minutes or longer are by no means rare. One study of 33,600 alarm calls in Los Angeles showed an average response time in the ten-to-twenty-minute range. But averages can be misleading. One study showed that for 15 percent of the calls, it took police *more than an hour* to arrive. If authorities respond within ten minutes, there's a reasonable chance of an apprehension; otherwise, chances of capture are slim. No matter what the response time, the deterrence and "on notice" factors are still important. But keep the response-time issue in mind when considering whether an alarm system is worth it to you.

• *The plague of false alarms.* No doubt about it, up to 90 percent of alarm calls are false alarms. False alarms may result from owner error, equipment malfunction, or detector oversensitivity (e.g., reactions to rattling windows). Alarm installers say false alarms are almost always caused by owner error, but other studies suggest that equipment malfunctions and oversensitivity are more common than industry spokespeople care to admit. Of course, no owner is perfect and no system is fail-safe. A certain proportion of false alarms is inevitable, and some alarms judged "false" by police may have been attempted break-ins, where the system scared off the burglar.

Police and other monitors say they respond to alarms as quickly as possible, despite the high false-alarm rate. But the tale of the boy who cried "Wolf!" suggests that they'd respond more quickly if there were fewer false alarms. False alarms also increase the tax burden on the 97 percent of homeowners and renters who do not have alarms. A San Francisco study showed that calls from the city's estimated 25,000 alarm systems consume 168 police hours a day, of which 165 are spent responding to false alarms. That's the equivalent of twenty officers doing nothing but answering false alarms. Police time is expensive. The cost of false alarms has prompted many communities to require alarm-installation permits ($10 to $50). Some police departments fine owners for over a certain number of false alarms a year ($25 to $50), and some charge owners for every call.

The false-alarm plague has persuaded many police that burglar alarms are more trouble than they're worth: "Alarms are good when they work," San Francisco Crime Prevention Officer Thomas Del Toore says, "but our emphasis is on the basics: good locks, strong doors, and locking up," in other words, first- and second-line precautions.

On-site-bell false alarms also annoy neighbors—a serious problem because neighborhood cooperation is crucial to their effectiveness. Alarm monitors have a duty to respond to every call, but neighbors are under no such obligation. I once lived across the street from a home with an on-site-bell system built around motion detectors. The wind rattled the windows, which set the system off regularly, much to the chagrin of everyone in the area. At first neighbors called the police promptly, but over time resentment grew. Some neighbors mentioned the problem to the owner, but he seemed unconcerned. As a result, people stopped calling and started seething. Several times the bell rang for the full fifteen minutes before it shut itself off. The police finally threatened not to respond to more calls until the owner changed his sensor system. That proved persuasive and the false alarms stopped, but it took quite a while for neighborhood resentment to subside. Owners of on-site-bell systems have a responsibility to eliminate false alarms, both as a courtesy to their neighbors and to ensure prompt reporting if the bell sounds.

• Cost-effectiveness. Burglar alarms should be considered only after your home has been carefully target-hardened. Then take stock of what you own, and figure what more it would cost to secure your peace of mind. If you decide to purchase an alarm system, authorities recommend a professionally installed combination system. Spokespeople for the National Burglar and Fire Alarm Association concede that their industry is "totally unregulated" and not without its con artists. They recommend dealing with companies in business for "no less than five years, and the longer the better." It's also best to visit the monitoring station, and to talk with alarm owners who use the service.

IF SOMEONE BREAKS IN WHILE YOU'RE GONE

Merely marking valuables may make little or no difference, but other simple, inexpensive steps minimize theft losses:

• *Secure valuables in place.* Televisions and stereos that are rarely moved can be secured with small screws. The idea is not to bolt them down permanently but to reduce their "grabability." If your television sits on a rolling stand, it can be attached to it. A burglar might unscrew it, but in addition to time and work, it would take a tool he probably wouldn't have. He might steal it, stand and all, but then he'd have to maneuver a large, awkward object. Faced with these problems, most burglars would move on to something easier to grab. Firearms should be kept unloaded, fitted with trigger locks, and stored in locked cabinets. It's also a good idea to lock tool cabinets.

• *Hide them.* Burglars are young, in a hurry, and usually intoxicated. They give the house a quick once-over, then leave. It's not difficult to hide valuables where burglars wouldn't look for them. Hiding places need not be elaborate. Just locate poorly lighted areas above or below normal eye level that would escape an anxious young man's notice. You know your home better than anyone else. Attics, basements, garages, linen and broom closets, kitchen cabinets, even the refrigerator, all have attractive stash possibilities. Cash can be kept in books, files, or envelopes taped behind calendars or picture frames. Jewelry may be stashed in linen closets, paint cans, or in old clothes. Use your imagination.

• *Consider prefabricated stashes.* In most homes, simple, out-of-the-way hiding places should suffice, but more elaborate alternatives are also available. The Hidden Wall Safe looks like an electrical outlet, but behind the face plate (easily removed with one turn of a screw) lie 35 cubic inches of secret storage space. That's not much, but the compartment can hold cash and jewelry. Placed at baseboard level, it's well below normal sight lines, and for added protection you can place it behind furniture or insert a dummy electrical plug. If you'd rather not cut a compartment into an old book, there's the Fake Book Safe.

If you're inclined toward do-it-yourself projects, the possibilities are truly limitless. Secure yet easily accessible hiding places can be constructed under rugs or floors, behind baseboards, or inside closets or furniture. Those interested should consult *The Stash Book*, the best source of creative concealment ideas. On the other hand, most valuables can be secured without resorting to prefabricated or custom stashes.

• *Vault boxes.* An inexpensive way to secure seldom-needed valuables, particularly important papers, is to rent a safe-deposit box at a bank. Small ones cost about $10 a year. Some banks provide them free to depositors.

• *Real safes.* Most people don't need a safe. But if the considerable investment (even for a used one) feels worth it, many are available. Popular models include the classic behind-the-picture-frame model and safes disguised to look like end tables. See "Safes" in the Yellow Pages.

IF AN INTRUDER IS THERE WHEN YOU RETURN

Do not enter. Examine the situation from a safe distance. If a vehicle is parked on your property, get a description and the license number. Then call the police or have a neighbor do so. Dial 911 (in most communities) and say, "Burglary in progress," at your address. A burglary "in progress" gets a faster police response than a burglary already completed. Don't go in until the police arrive or until you're certain the intruder has left. If you see him, take note of his escape direction and concentrate on getting a good description.

Don't try to be a hero. Ex-burglar Marcus Ratledge writes: "The worst thing is to catch a burglar in the act." Cornered burglars are among the most dangerous criminals. Most are terrified of confrontations. If armed, they often use their weapons. Even if not armed when they break in, they may well be by the time residents return. Every home contains knives, and burglars are quick to steal poorly secured firearms. The recommendation to avoid confrontations becomes even more important if your doors have double-cylinder locks,. which hinder a burglar's escape.

IF YOU'RE AWAKENED BY STRANGE NOISES

This is the situation everyone dreads. Good first- and second-line precautions should almost eliminate this possibility, but there's always some risk that a burglar—or rapist—might break in while you're home. What should you do? Options include:

• *Leave the house, call 911 and say, "Burglary in progress" at your address.* Avoid confrontations. Of course, if you're on the second floor and hear noises below, it may be impossible to leave. If you have children, it would be unthinkable to leave without them.

• *If you stay, call 911 and say, "Burglary in progress" at your address.* Don't panic. Be sure to give your address. Then try to scare the burglar away. Chances are he's a teenager. If lights go on, or someone shouts, "The police are on their way!" or a shriek alarm sounds, he may leave.

• *Install a lock on your bedroom door and keep a telephone extension there.* That way you can call the police in relative safety. You can still try to scare the intruder away from behind a locked door.

• *Firearms.* Opinion is passionately divided on the advisability of using firearms to defend against burglars, but half of U.S. homes are armed, and millions of people keep firearms in their bedrooms specifically for this eventuality.

Studies show that guns foil about 2 percent of burglaries of occupied homes. In 1980, the FBI collected reports of 3.75 million burglaries, but half go unreported, so the true number was probably closer to 7.5 million. Since half of all homes are armed, it's reasonable to presume that there were 3.75 million burglaries of armed households. If 10 percent of armed residents were home, and 2 percent of them successfully used their weapons, then private weaponry foiled approximately 7,500 burglaries in 1980.

If you own any firearms, be sure to study the Ten Commandments of Firearm Safety in chapter 11, specifically commandment five: "Know your target and backstop." *Never* shoot at anything you cannot see clearly. Every year people accidentally shoot loved ones or neighbors they mistake for burglars. *Never* shoot at anything without assessing what's *behind* your target. Every year people shoot innocent bystanders in the rooms—or homes—behind their targets. Even small caliber ammunition can travel through several walls. Also, store firearms unloaded, with trigger locks, in locked cabinets. Every year about four hundred American children die from injuries sustained while playing with inadequately secured weapons.

WHEN YOU'RE AWAY

In addition to locking up, setting the light timers, and dealing with the newspaper and mail, here are other vacation precautions security experts recommend:

• *Housesitters.* Try to arrange for someone you trust to live in your home while you're away. If that's not possible, ask a friend or two to stop by occasionally to take stock of things.

• *Hide more valuables.* Televisions and other valuables kept readily available when you're home can be stashed before you leave. Another approach is to schedule repair or maintenance work while you're away, and leave these objects at a repair shop.

• *Yard care.* On extended trips, make arrangements for yard care or snow shoveling. Untended property is a magnet for burglars.

• *Tell the police you'll be away.* Don't expect miracles. The larger your community, the less such a call will do. Some departments might divert officers to check on the homes of vacationing residents, but most cannot. Nonetheless, the department's prior knowledge that you'll be away may make a difference if they are called.

• *In hotels.* Hotel guests are at a considerable security disadvantage. Many people have access to your room, and it's difficult to hide valuables. So travel light, secure valuables on your person, and check valuables you'd rather not carry with the hotel management.

• *Consider a travel lock.* The Yale Travelok is a small sturdy lock for use on hotel (or home) dresser drawers while you're out, and hotel room doors when you're in. It weighs about six ounces and costs $15 at lock shops.

• *Security clothing.* Money, passports, and other small valuables can be concealed in shoes, socks, bras, or coat linings. *The Stash Book* lists more than fifty places where travelers can hide valuables in clothing or luggage. If you're interested in a money belt, money watchband, or secret pocket leg bands, see Resources.

JUST IN CASE: INSURANCE

Insurance is an integral part of property protection. For homeowners, theft insurance is included in overall homeowners' policies. For renters, insurance costs are shared: The owner insures the building, but tenants must insure their personal property.

Property insurance protects against losses from either "named perils" or "all risks." Basic named-perils policies cover losses from: fire or lightning, theft, vandalism, smoke, wind or hail, broken glass, motor vehicles, aircraft, explosions, and riots. "Broad-coverage named perils," typical of renters' policies, includes damage from: falling objects, ice and snow, collapse of building, overflow of water or steam, freezing, electrical wiring, and accidental cracking, e.g., a boiler. "All risk" coverage includes more perils (check the policy), but the name is misleading; it does not cover every possible source of damage. Catastrophes (floods, landslides, earthquakes, and so on) are excluded. Separate policies may be purchased to cover these risks.

Coverage limits and deductibles depend on the policy. Homeowners' policies typically cover the contents of the house (excluding motor vehicles) for an amount equal to half the home's total coverage. Renters' policies specify coverage limits.

For particular items, property policies specify coverage limits. These vary, but the following ranges are typical:

• currency and coin collections, $100–$200
• securities, deeds, and valuable papers, $500–$1,000
• boats, trailers, and boat motors, $500–$1,000
• jewelry, watches, and furs, $500–$1,000

- silverware and goldware, $1,000–$2,500
- firearms, $1,000–$2,000
- losses away from home, $1,000–$2,000
- losses due to check forgery or unauthorized use of credit cards, $500–$1,000

These items may be insured for more by purchasing extra coverage ("floaters") at additional cost.

When insuring property against crime-related losses or damage, shop for a policy that does not require proof of forced entry. As we have seen, more than a third of burglary losses do not involve forced entry. Also, insure your property for replacement value not cash value. Replacement coverage costs about 15 percent more, but it's worth it. Cash value means original cost minus annual depreciation. Items owned for more than a few years have relatively small cash values.

To collect on a theft-loss claim, you must report the loss promptly to the police. If you notice other items missing after the initial report, you may amend it. The best way to file a complete initial report and minimize reimbursement problems is to keep an inventory of your valuables, with photographs where appropriate. Update it periodically and keep an extra copy in a safe place, preferably a bank vault, where it's protected from fire. (For information on theft-related income tax deductions, see chapter 8.)

Consumer Reports surveyed 280,000 readers about their experiences with insurance. Based on their feelings of satisfaction with the way all claims (not just crime-related claims) were handled, the magazine rated thirty of the largest companies in its September 1980 issue (available at libraries or check the annual *Buying Guide*).

In some high-risk and/or low-income areas, property insurance may be beyond the means of many residents. Fortunately, Federal Crime Insurance is available to many homeowners, renters, and businesses. The residential program requires at least dead bolts on doors and clamshell clasps on windows. It costs $120 a year for $10,000 coverage, with a deductible of $100 or 5 percent of the loss, whichever is greater. The commercial program requires an alarm system (different systems depending on the business). Business premiums and deductibles are based on sales.

HOW TO REPORT A BURGLARY

Don't be surprised if the police take their time arriving; "completed" burglaries are a low priority for most departments. When the officers appear:

• *Be reasonable.* Don't expect them to apprehend anyone. In 1980, police made arrests in just 14 percent of reported burglaries. The primary responsibility for burglary prevention falls on residents to keep intruders out, not on police to catch them after they've gotten in.

• *Get the officers' names.* Ask whom you should call if you discover any additional losses, or if you obtain additional information about the burglary from neighbors.

• *Be persistent without becoming obnoxious.* About 8 percent of stolen property is eventually returned. Check in periodically with the police. There's a chance you might recover something.

INSURANCE FOR TARGET-HARDENED HOMES ONLY?

Burglary losses come to more than $3 billion a year, and the insurance industry estimates that index crimes cost the typical family, whether victimized or not, more than $3,000 a year in insurance premiums, repair and replacement costs, and taxes to finance the criminal justice system.

✓ Few things fuel the impulse to commit burglary as much as previously successful break-ins; therefore, every burglary contributes to future ones, and we all have an interest in keeping intruders not only out of our own homes but *every* home.

It is abundantly clear that first- and second-line defenses reduce burglary risk 70 to 80 percent. It's equally clear that, despite the obvious benefit, millions of homes are inadequately protected. Given the staggering costs involved, it's certainly in the national interest to encourage people to target-harden their homes. One relatively painless way to do this would be governmental prohibition of the insurance industry from providing theft coverage for homes that do not have a certificate showing that the owner has implemented the recommendations of a police security survey. There is already precedent for this: Federal Crime Insurance requires dead bolt locks on doors and clamshell clasps on windows. Why not expand this to include all theft insurance? As an added incentive, homeowners' and landlords' investments in security hardware could be tax-deductible.

This approach would significantly reduce the number of burglaries. It would also encourage greater crime-prevention awareness and increase the nation's police commitment to proactive efforts. It would help everyone become much safer.

Resources:

The Complete Book of Locks, Keys, Burglar
and Smoke Alarms, and Other Security Devices
by Eugene A. Sloane
1977, 320 pages, $7.95
William Morrow & Co.
Wilmor Warehouse
6 Henderson Drive
West Caldwell, NJ 07006

The Stash Book
by Peter Hjersman
1978, 120 pages, $4.95
And/Or Press
P.O. Box 2246
Berkeley, CA 94702

The Hidden Wall Safe
$13.20 postpaid
Nora Nelson, Dept. OOATV
621 Avenue of the Americas
New York, NY 10011

The Fake Book Safe
$19.50 postpaid
Brookstone Co.
127 Vose Farm Rd.
Peterborough, NH 03458

Money Belts
$20–$25 postpaid
Western Manufacturing Co., Inc.
149 Ninth St.
San Francisco, CA 94103

Money Watchband
$9.00 postpaid
The Pleasure Chest
20 West 20th St.
New York, NY 10011

"Sok-It-Away" secret pocket leg band
$8.50 postpaid
Komfort Carrier, Inc.
P.O. Box 638
Turlock, CA 95380

"Crime Prevention Program"
The National Retired Teachers Association/
American Association of Retired Persons
see Resources, chapter 4.

Federal Crime Insurance
P.O. Box 41033
Bethesda, MD 41033
(800) 638–8780

Available in: Alabama, Arkansas, California, Colorado, Connecticut, Delaware, Florida, Georgia, Illinois, Iowa, Kansas, Louisiana, Maryland, Massachusetts, Minnesota, Missouri, New Jersey, New Mexico, New York, North Carolina, Ohio, Pennsylvania, Rhode Island, Tennessee, Virginia, Washington, and Wisconsin, the District of Columbia, Puerto Rico, and the Virgin Islands.

6

How to Prevent Other Theft Crimes

AUTO BURGLARY: YOU'RE ON YOUR OWN

Of all street crimes, auto burglary is the least likely to be challenged by passersby, *including police*. This comes from Harold Takooshian, a professor of social psychology at Fordham University in New York, who from 1977 to 1980 studied the reactions of pedestrians in eight cities to auto burglary. Takooshian's assistants posed as thieves and "broke into" three hundred parked cars with visible valuables inside. Of the eight thousand pedestrians who walked past the break-ins, fewer than a thousand even noticed them, and only 4.5 percent challenged the "thief" in any way. In fact, pedestrians, including police, were three times more likely to *help* than hinder the thieves.

Why were pedestrians more likely to help than challenge auto burglars? Largely because of the widespread belief that crime involves stealth. Takooshian's researchers attempted their break-ins openly, in broad daylight, on crowded streets. When interviewed later, a few of those who noticed the break-ins said they "felt funny" about them, but most said they assumed the car belonged to the "thief," even when he looked scruffy and smashed a window to gain entry. Several police were among those who assisted the break-ins, and *not one* asked for the "burglar's" driver's license or registration.

A parked car is completely anonymous. It can't call for help and only in rare instances does anyone in the immediate vicinity know who owns it. As far as auto burglary is concerned, owners are on their own. Fortunately, this crime is not difficult to prevent:

• *Keep valuables out of sight.* This is by far the most important recommendation. Auto burglars, usually teens, don't break in just for the hell of it. They smash a window because they see something valuable inside. Even if you leave your car only briefly, lock valuables in the trunk. If that's not possible, hide them under an old blanket kept in the car for this purpose. Tape decks can sometimes be concealed in glove compartments or by maps, hats, gloves, or phony AM-radio face plates, and special locks have been developed to secure them in place. Tape decks should also be insured. Check your policy. Some automatically cover them; others require an additional premium, usually about $20 a year.

• *Lock up, even in your own driveway or garage.* In some places, this may not be necessary, but it's always prudent, especially with the trend toward rapid population growth in nonmetropolitan areas. Locking up also deters vehicle theft.

• *Replace "flared post" inside lock buttons with the tapered variety.* This largely prevents unlocking from the outside with a coat hanger.

• *Consider an auto burglar alarm.* Auto alarms have some of the advantages of home systems, but more of the disadvantages. Most come with perimeter stickers which will deter some break-ins, and the alarm's noise may thwart others. But even with an alarm, if a briefcase or camera is visible inside, a thief can often break a window, grab the item, and be blocks away before anyone calls the police. An alarm is no substitute for hiding valuables and locking up.

Not all auto alarms are *burglar* alarms; some only protect against vehicle theft. To deter burglary, an auto alarm should have glass sensors to detect window tampering and/or motion sensors to detect movement inside the vehicle.

AUTO THEFT: REDUCE RISK UP TO 85 PERCENT

Motor vehicle theft is the most paradoxical property crime. FBI and census data agree that the auto-theft rate has been "generally stable since 1971." But beneath the surface, auto theft, which costs the nation $3.2 billion a year, has undergone a transformation more profound than any other street crime.

During the 1960s, joy-riding teens did the vast majority of the stealing, and 90 percent of stolen cars were recovered. Today, young people still account for most vehicle theft, but the recovery rate has dropped by almost half, to 55 percent. Each year nearly 500,000 cars, vans, and trucks disappear for good, usually into "chop shops" that dismantle them to supply the enormous demand for stolen parts. The upshot is that risk of auto theft may have remained about the same during the past decade, but the stakes have increased considerably.

Why the change? Why the chop shops? Several reasons: The 55-mile-an-hour speed limit, more crash-resistant bumper designs, and more severe penalties for drunk driving have reduced the number of highway accidents, with the result that fewer cars become sources for legal parts. In addition, the economic problems of recent years have forced many people to keep their cars longer. Instead of buying new cars, people replace parts. Used parts are cheaper than new ones, and when "used" parts are stolen, dealer profits increase and prices may be even lower.

Recall that a car owner's risk of auto theft varies with place of residence, age, and race. It's highest in cities, lower in the suburbs, and lowest in rural areas. Those under twenty-one are almost *nine times* as likely to be victimized as those over sixty-five, and black people and Hispanics have twice the risk of whites.

The car itself also affects theft risk. The Highway Loss Data Institute (HLDI), an insurance industry group in Washington, D.C., reports that subcompacts are at lowest risk, while bigger "sexier" cars are at highest risk (except station wagons, which are at lower risk than comparable sedans). Based on ratios for each model of cars stolen to cars on the road through 1981, the HLDI compiled the following lists of the ten cars most likely and least likely to be stolen. The numbers in parentheses indicate relative risk. Average risk is set at 100. A relative risk of 400 means the likelihood of the car being stolen is four times the average. A relative risk of 25 means one-fourth the average risk. The ten most likely targets included:

- BMW 320i (relative risk, 895)
- Chevrolet Corvette (686)
- Ford Thunderbird (590)
- Porsche 924 (460)
- Chevrolet Caprice Classic two-door (425)
- Ford LTD four-door (392)
- Mercury Marquis two-door (391)
- Volkswagen Rabbit Scirocco (313)
- Pontiac Bonneville two-door (303)
- Lincoln Mark VI (300)

The ten least likely targets were:

- Dodge Omni four-door (relative risk, 18)
- Chevrolet Citation four-door (18)
- Dodge Colt two-door (19)
- Plymouth Champ two-door (21)
- Ford Escort two-door (23)
- Plymouth Horizon four-door (23)
- Chevrolet Citation two-door (25)
- Chevrolet Chevette four-door (27)
- Buick Skylark two- and four-door (33)
- Ford Fiesta two-door (35)

Despite the differences in victim- and vehicle-based risk, authorities such as Marcus Ratledge, who stole cars for a multimillion-dollar auto-theft ring, agree that simple precautions reduce risk up to 85 percent:

- *Lock up.* Nearly one stolen car in five is left unlocked, many with the key in the ignition.
- *Try to park in open, lighted areas.* Opportunities for concealment mean increased risk of theft.

• *Do not use magnetic spare key boxes.* These are as hazardous as leaving a housekey under the doormat.

• *Do not keep your proof of ownership ("pink slip") in the vehicle.* Thieves can use it to sell the car.

• *Park with front wheels turned sharply.* This helps prevent towing.

• *When buying, look for a car with an inside hood release.* This deters battery theft and "hot-wiring," bypassing the ignition system to start the car directly from the starter motor. If your hood release is on the hood, consider a hood lock. Gasoline caps that lock are also a good idea.

• *Everyone's FREE superlock.* Simply remove the distributor rotor (see figure 6–1). This trick has almost every advantage. It's quick, simple, effective, and best of all, *free.* Just snap off the distributor cap and remove the T-shaped part that sits in the middle of the distributor. Once removed, the rotor fits easily into a purse, briefcase, or the trunk. Without the rotor, the car cannot start. Very few car thieves are given to mechanical troubleshooting, and even if one located the problem, how many carry spare rotors? The one disadvantage of rotor removal is that the "lock" is invisible from outside the car.

• *Superlocks.* These are highly visible. Even if the hood is locked, a car thief might still yank out the ignition lock, then flip the exposed switch to start the car. With an in-column ignition, an "armor collar" can be locked around the steering column to secure the ignition lock. With an in-dash ignition, you might consider a "crook lock," an S-shaped device that locks around the steering wheel and brake pedal to prevent a thief from driving the car even if he starts it. These locks will slow any thief and, as a result, deter a good many (around $50).

Extra ignition switches, called "disablers," also deter hot-wiring. Disablers prevent the car from starting unless the additional well-hidden ignition switch is thrown. For information, check with auto electrical shops (about $50–$75 installed).

• *Auto theft alarms.* Good ones cost in the $150 to $400 range. Among the many on the market, the Chapman systems are frequently recommended. The Chapman Black Panther features a hood lock, an ignition disabler, and other antitampering devices that

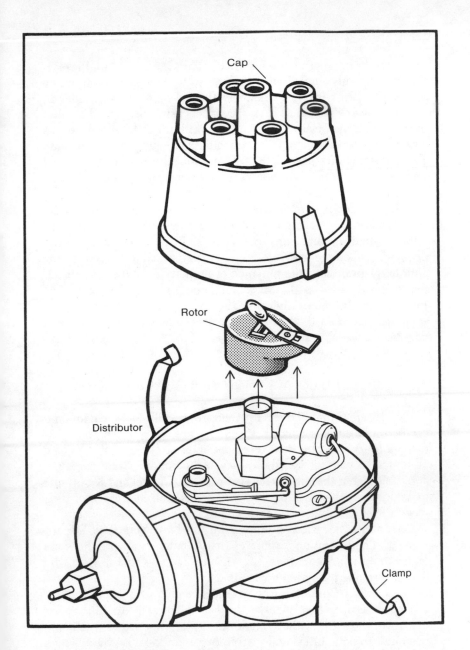

Cap

Rotor

Distributor

Clamp

Figure 6-1: Everyone's Free Superlock

125

set off the horn (about $200 installed). The Chapman Total Protection System adds burglary-prevention features (glass and motion sensors) to the Black Panther (about $400 installed). It also includes an optional paging device. Pagers are pocket-size beepers that alert owners when their alarms sound. They work for distances of up to a half mile in open country, less in cities. If you invest in an auto alarm, systems with pagers are best. Without this feature, you might find your car broken into—not by thieves but by police called by residents to turn off the siren.

• *A note about auto insurance.* "Comprehensive" coverage insures against vehicle theft, and any damage sustained during attempted thefts or auto burglaries. Most policies have a $50 or $100 deductible. Comprehensive does not cover valuables stolen during auto burglaries; that's the province of property insurance. Theft settlements are based on the car's blue book (i.e., depreciated) value. Few policies automatically cover the cost of renting a replacement car if damage from theft or burglary necessitates repair work. Such coverage is available at added cost.

BICYCLE LOCKS WITH $250 GUARANTEES

Bicycles are favorite targets for theft. Many bike locks, chains, and cables can be cut in seconds with bolt cutters. Once stolen, bikes are difficult to identify and easy to repaint and sell. Short of stationing a rabid dog by your ten-speed, no bicycle-protection system can guarantee safety, but the companies that produce Citadel and Kryptonite locks do the next best thing: If a thief steals a bike with one of their locks, they'll reimburse you up to $250.

Larry Reilly, bicycle coordinator for the New York City Department of Transportation, estimates that Citadel or Kryptonite locks reduce theft risk "more than 30 percent." He says that anyone who doesn't use one is "asking for trouble."

Top-rated by *Consumer Reports,* Citadel and Kryptonite locks are U-shaped devices that shackle the bicycle directly to bike racks, fences, and so forth, without chains or cable. They are "virtually impervious" to bolt cutters and feature Ace cylindrical keyways, which are relatively pick-resistant (though lock-picking is even rarer among bike thieves than among burglars). When not in use, they fit conveniently into a bracket easily mounted inside the bike frame. Both locks cost around $30 at bike shops (or see Resources). The Master Company recently introduced a similar bike lock and guarantee.

CON GAMES: HOW TO AVOID THE "STING"

Everyone likes a "deal," and even prudent people can begin to salivate at opportunities that promise "easy money tax-free." No matter whether the motivation is bargain hunting or greed, too often the result is a con game. There are no reliable fraud statistics, but authorities agree that it costs Americans more money every year than *all index crimes combined.*

Yet fraud has always been a low priority for law enforcement. The burglar who walks off with your $500 television is more likely to go to jail than the con man who walks off with $10,000 of your savings. Fraud rarely inspires lurid headlines, police medals for valor, political campaign promises, or national anxiety attacks. It's a quiet, nonviolent crime. But the trauma of being "taken" can be every bit as unnerving as armed robbery.

More than other crimes, fraud involves victim participation. Con artists exploit victims' desire for easy, often legally questionable gain. Prosecutors sometimes say there are two criminals in the typical fraud, the one who takes the money and the one who gives it. As a result, it's much more embarrassing to fall victim to fraud than to most other crimes. Victims see themselves, often correctly, as "suckers." They are often reluctant to file complaints because legal action may involve admitting participation in transactions of dubious legality. Victims' reluctance to step forward is an added advantage for the con artist. In addition, the public attitude toward fraud victims has never been charitable. In business, the assumption is that "it's a jungle out there," and if some people get burned, well, they just weren't sufficiently wary. To be sure, there are limits; everyone deplores "stealing from widows and orphans." But P. T. Barnum summarized the prevailing perspective on fraud in a remark that has become as American as apple pie: "Never give a sucker an even break."

Recently, the consumer movement has begun to change that view.

But while law enforcement commitment to fighting fraud has increased, those in the field say consumer-protection efforts have been more than offset by the rapid growth of the economy's service sector. As services grow increasingly numerous and complex, so do opportunities for fraud.

My brother Steven has worked for many years as a prosecutor for the San Francisco D.A.'s Consumer Fraud Unit. A complete discussion of fraud is beyond the scope of this book, but Steven and other authorities in the field offer these insights: There are two basic kinds of fraud. One involves wholly illegitimate businesses (con games); the other, legitimate businesses that may use illegitimate practices (consumer fraud).

The classic fraud is the land swindle: "You can make a fortune with a small investment in my diamond mine in Arizona." These days, land-fraud schemes are more likely to promise big returns on condominium time-share arrangements, but the result is the same—you never see your money again. Even if the swindler is convicted and ordered to make restitution, chances are you'll never get a penny. No court can force con artists to return money they don't have, and when brought to trial they *never* have enough to make restitution. Con artists very rarely go to jail, and even when they do, they almost never draw more than one year. The upshot is that we must protect ourselves from con games.

Like street assaults, con games follow a pattern. The stages include:

• *The Bait.* The swindler grabs your attention with a chance to make easy money quickly.

• *The Hook.* To take advantage of this fabulous opportunity, you must produce a good deal of cash at once. When you hesitate to deal in cash, the con man says it's one of the beauties of the deal—without checks, there are no bank records, therefore no need to report the income to the IRS; your earnings will be tax-free!

• *The Sting.* You hand over the money.

• *The Stall.* Your connection is terribly sorry, there has been a delay. But not to worry, everything is fine. . . . Other delays follow.

• *The End.* Your connection disappears. You don't want to admit it, but you realize you've been duped.

Con games come in infinite varieties but most follow the pattern outlined above and all involve cash. Anyone is fair game, but older people are frequent targets. Those on fixed incomes may find offers of easy tax-free income or tremendous savings on necessary items (like hearing aids) too good to pass up, especially when they come from attractive young women who seem so sweet and sincere. Some classic con games include:

• *The Bank Examiner.* An "investigator" says you can help trap a dishonest bank employee—and reap a sizable reward—by withdrawing cash from your account and turning it over to him. The con man advises absolute secrecy and plays on the romance of this rare opportunity.

• *The Pigeon Drop.* The swindler "finds" a bundle of cash, then convinces you that you can share in it by withdrawing some of your own money and giving it to him as a "good faith deposit."

• *The Fence.* The con artist says he can get you a new TV at a fraction of its retail price. The merchandise is stolen, but cannot be traced. All you have to do is put up the cash so he can pick it up. Then you never see him again, or he tells you he was "robbed." This swindle is particularly effective because victims rarely report it to the police. They fear prosecution for attempting to buy "hot" merchandise.

• *The Funeral Chaser.* A rather embarrassed "salesman" appears at the home of a recently bereaved victim with an expensive piece of jewelry or another item, claiming that the deceased put a down payment on it and that the victim "owes" the balance.

There are two basic recommendations for avoiding swindles: Beware of deals that sound too good to be true, and *never deal in cash.*

HOW TO AVOID CONSUMER FRAUD

A good deal of fraud results from illegal practices by legitimate businesses. Most businesspeople are honest, but many businesses provide opportunities to mislead customers and make easy money.

The most prevalent illegal practice is the "bait-and-switch": A store advertises a trememdous discount on one product to attract shoppers. Salespeople then subtly maneuver them into buying a similar, higher profit item, often with apologies that the advertised product is sold out. Bait-and-switch scams are particularly common in televisions, stereos, and home computers, where even informed shoppers can be snowed by salespeople's apparent command of technical terms. But they are by no means rare in other big-ticket items: cars, refrigerators, furniture, and so on. You can reduce your risk of bait-and-switch operations in several ways:

• *Do your homework.* Before making any major purchase, ask friends and others who own the product about desirable features, maintenance and repair problems, good brands, and good stores. Check *Consumer Reports'* annual *Buying Guide* ($3.50 at most bookstores).

• *Shop slowly.* Impulse purchases carry the highest risk. Don't succumb to pressure from salespeople or advertisements that say "Buy NOW! Sale Ends Today." There's always another sale.

• *Call consumer agencies.* Most states have Departments of Consumer Affairs. Public agency personnel are rarely permitted to say: "Don't shop at X," but they can still provide good information and referrals. Many communities have consumer action organizations, nonprofit groups that promote consumer interests. Many discuss businesses by name.

An increasing number of Better Business Bureaus (BBB) also name names. It's important to understand that BBBs are financed by local businesses. In the past, BBBs were largely public-relations fronts for local Chambers of Commerce. They would take consumers' complaints, not to be advocates for them, but to encourage people to vent their anger without calling the district attorney. Some BBBs still provide largely sham complaint services—and only the naive could expect them to move assertively on complaints against their major contributors—but in recent years BBBs have begun to change for the better, especially in communities with active consumer organizations. Enlightened BBBs understand that shoddy business practices reflect badly on *all* businesses. An increasing number will discuss complaints on file, and whether any have been referred to the district attorney.

Beyond bait-and-switch operations, consumer fraud authorities warn that home-improvement and auto-repair disputes lead to many complaints. Most contractors and mechanics are honest and do good work, but to prevent problems:

• *Get recommendations.* Satisfied customers are your best assurance of quality work.

• *Licensing.* It's best to use licensed contractors and repair people. There is a tendency to say, "He's not licensed, therefore, he'll be cheaper." Possibly, and many unlicensed people do good work. But the license means that consumers have at least some recourse to a public agency in the event of problems. Of course, no license guarantees quality work, which is why recommendations are so important.

• *Get written estimates before work begins.*

• *Set payment terms before work begins.* Ideally, arrange for a deposit, then for further payments as the work progresses.

• *Get receipts.*

PREVENTING CRIME IN THE COUNTRY

Loss of community cohesion is a prime cause of crime. Crime has always been a problem in "boom towns," instant communities with substantial transience and little stability. Even in areas with relatively little poverty and unemployment—for example, Sunbelt cities in the mid-1970s—crime rates rose sharply because rapid population growth disrupted community stability. This is one reason why historically crime has clustered in urban areas. For the past 150 years, American cities have been the nation's fastest-growing communities. Now, for the first time since 1820, rural and small-town America is growing faster than the cities. Nonmetropolitan areas grew by 15 percent during the 1970s compared to an urban population *decline* of five percent. According to census surveys, rural residents are 45 percent less likely than urban dwellers to fall victim to violent crime, and 35 percent less likely to suffer theft. The relative safety of the country has been a major attraction for urban refugees, but this may change as rural communities continue to grow faster than the cities.

The guidelines for target-hardening country homes and farm buildings parallel those already discussed. But rural residents, especially farmers, have other property attractive to thieves: farm equipment, livestock, bees, timber, and so on. The National Rural Crime Prevention Center provides information on rural security concerns in its series of excellent "Home and Farm Security Bulletins."

BEYOND THE FORTRESS MENTALITY

Locking up and other crime-prevention recommendations substantially reduce risk of victimization. But individual efforts are only part of becoming safer. Street awareness and target-hardening can become grim affairs when you feel you're a "lone ranger" battling a hostile world full of criminals. Although most crimes are the work of young men who live in the general vicinity, criminals comprise only a tiny fraction of any community's residents. Most people face the same risks as their neighbors, and are open to crime-prevention efforts.

It's certainly important to lock up, but it's just as important to *open up* to those around you. Cooperative efforts build community cohesion, a crucial element in crime prevention. Neighborhood Watch in Detroit is just one of many programs that have reduced crime substantially in many communities. These programs are the subject of the next chapter.

RESOURCES:

Chapman Auto Alarms
Chapman Industries
2638 United Lane
Elk Grove, IL 60007

Citadel Bicycle Lock
Bike Security Systems
177 Tosca Dr.
Stoughton, MA 02072

Kryptonite Bicycle Lock
95 Freeport St.
Boston, MA 02122

National Rural Crime Prevention Center
(Ohio State University)
2120 Fyffe Rd.
Columbus, OH 43210

"Crime Prevention Handbook for Senior Citizens"
National Institute on Law Enforcement and
Criminal Justice, U.S. Dept. of Justice
1977, 53 pages, $2.10
U.S. Government Bookstores
or by mail
Superintendent of Documents
U.S. Government Printing Office
Washington, DC 20402
Stock No. 027-000-00589-0

"Crime Prevention Program"
National Retired Teachers Association/
American Association of Retired Persons
See Resources for chapter 4.

7

Neighbor to Neighbor: Crime Prevention through Community Self-Help

THE VICTIM AMERICA CANNOT FORGET

Kitty Genovese. Her image still haunts the nation's conscience twenty years after she was raped and murdered in Queens, New York. At 3:20 A.M. on March 13, 1964, twenty-eight-year-old Catherine Genovese returned home to Kew Gardens from her job as the manager of a nearby bar. She parked her car at the Long Island Railroad station and started to walk the two blocks to her apartment on Austin Street.

At the time, Kew Gardens was a quiet, middle-class neighborhood of single-family homes, with a few apartments near the rail line. It was a good neighborhood, a low-crime area. As Genovese walked up the street, twenty-nine-year-old Winston Moseley jumped out of his car, grabbed her, and stabbed her four times. Genovese screamed, "Oh my God! Somebody help me!"

The myth is that no one did. Thirty-eight people heard her cries, but no one called the police for thirty minutes. The Genovese killing is often cited as evidence that people "don't want to get involved." Kitty Genovese was *not* ignored. Two people tried to help her. Their gestures reflected an ignorance of crime-prevention skills, and after her death, they felt as ashamed as their thirty-six neighbors who did nothing. Nevertheless, their attempts to assist Genovese very nearly saved her life.

When she first screamed for help, a light flashed on in the apartment building across the street. A man stuck his head out a window and yelled, "Leave that girl alone!" Amazingly, Moseley did. He broke off his attack and returned to his car. Genovese, injured but still conscious, staggered to the vestibule of her building, then collapsed.

Moseley waited in his car. No one appeared on the street. No other lights came on. At his trial, he said, "It was 3 A.M. and cold. I had the feeling that man would go back to sleep." He did. Only then did Moseley return to his victim. He found Genovese, stabbed her eight more times, and sexually assaulted her.

Moseley's second attack roused another neighbor, but he did not call the police. He called a friend and told him what he thought might be happening. The friend urged him to call the police, which he did, finally, at 3:50, a half hour after Genovese's first cry.

When the police arrived, they found Genovese still alive, but she died on the way to the hospital. They told reporters that if the call had come in just a few minutes earlier, she would have survived.

Could a similar crime happen elsewhere? Of course. In 1980 alone, more than 144,000 Americans were assaulted with knives, and 4,000 of them died. Could dozens of people hear a woman scream late at night and allow thirty minutes to elapse before even one of them called the police? Perhaps. But in a large and growing number of communities the response would be much different. It *was different* in a tough neighborhood of Philadelphia in 1975. But that's getting ahead of the story.

THE BIRTH OF NEIGHBORHOOD WATCH

Ellie Wegener says she "never even *heard* of community organizing" before she started doing it. After five years in England, she moved to Philadelphia in 1968 when her husband, a Lutheran minister, took a job at the University of Pennsylvania.

The family settled near the university in West Philadelphia, one of the city's most heterogeneous—and crime-ridden—neighborhoods. Some residents were well off, but most were not. "We had all kinds," Wegener recalls, "blacks, whites, Hispanics, recent immigrants, elderly people, and university students, with some staff families like ours thrown in. The area was also badly run down. Most of the yards were untended. We could feel how estranged people were from each other." Still, the neighborhood suited the Wegeners. "My husband wanted to be accessible to the students he worked with, and many of them lived there. We were also 'urban people.' Despite the problems, we liked the diversity of the area."

One afternoon in 1971, Ellie returned home to the news that her close friend across the street had just been raped. She rushed over and heard the story. Her friend was unlocking her door, arms laden with groceries, when suddenly a young man jumped out of the bushes, forced his way inside, then beat and raped her. He told her that if she called the police, he would return and kill her.

The victim reported the assault to the police, but refused to return home for fear that the rapist might carry out his threat. She and her family moved in temporarily with the Wegeners.

The newspapers reported that this "grocery rapist" had struck twice during the previous two weeks within a few blocks of his attack on Ellie's friend. In each case, he had overpowered women with shopping bags as they unlocked their front doors.

Ellie felt petrified. "Homes burglarized, people afraid to go out, muggings in broad daylight—and now this! If I'd arrived home a little earlier, it could have been me." But she also felt something else, determination to help. "I couldn't believe that something like that could happen so close to me. By then I knew several people on our block, and I invited them over to talk about helping my friend. That was all I wanted to do, help her. I didn't have the foggiest idea about crime prevention, but word got around that I was doing something about crime, and forty people showed up."

The participants at that first meeting were a cross-section of the neighborhood, people very different from one another. "Many had been neighbors for years," Wegener recalls, "but they'd never met. At first, people didn't trust each other. But despite their differences, they had identical concerns about crime. As they shared their feelings about the rapes, their mistrust began to subside."

Wegener had no program in mind. "I didn't see that first meeting as community organizing; to me, it was common sense. I didn't have a plan. The plan emerged from the group. The grocery rapist operated in a very small area, just a few blocks. We decided to focus on that small area and work block by block. We had seven blocks represented. We decided to convene individual block meetings to talk about the rapist, then meet back together the following month."

THE FIRST SECURITY SURVEYS—
BY AN EX-BURGLAR

At its second meeting, the group was larger. The seven block meetings had been well attended because of the rape crisis, and people from neighboring blocks were eager to participate. The block meetings had drawn up lists of needs that turned out to be quite similar: crime-prevention information, improved relations with the police, and the capture of the grocery rapist.

No one in the block groups knew much about crime prevention. Then one man stepped forward to share his expertise. "He was an ex-burglar who lived in a nearby Quaker halfway house," Wegener recalls. "He was in his thirties, and recently released from prison. People would have been scared of him, except that he was staying with the Quakers, which made him okay. Actually, we felt lucky to have the benefit of his experience. We had no other crime experts. You have to remember, this was 1971, several years before police departments did crime-prevention work as we understand it today. I'll never forget the meeting when this ex-burglar took everyone on a tour of my house and pointed out all the ways he could break in. It was our first 'security survey.' The suggestions he made would be considered typical target-hardening advice today, but back then they were a revelation."

The block groups were eager for crime-prevention advice, so Ellie launched "The Blockbuilder," a neighborhood newsletter filled with crime-prevention tips. Soon people were target-hardening their homes, trimming their shrubs, greeting their neighbors, and keeping an eye on the community. Within a few months, people in the block groups began to feel safer.

West Philadelphia's block groups soon attracted media attention. "After the word got out, I started getting calls from real estate brokers. At first I wondered why so many realtors were interested in our work. Then it hit me: Property values were going up. I was writing and speaking about our program, and the realtors were capitalizing on it. People would say, 'If I'm going to live in West Philadelphia, I want a place in that area where the people are fighting crime.' If I'd been in real estate back then instead of crime prevention, I'd be rich today."

THE BLOCK GROUPS CAPTURE THE GROCERY RAPIST

When the block groups moved to improve relations with the police, the local captain was more than cooperative. He had tried to hold meetings where neighborhood people could meet local officers, but no residents ever attended. This frustrated him and hurt officer morale. Then the block groups asked him to send some officers to their meetings. He responded enthusiastically, and police-community relations began to improve, at least on the local level.

Officials at police headquarters, however, opposed the organizing effort, especially the neighborhood's eagerness to help capture the grocery rapist. They believed that apprehending criminals was best left to the professionals. "At first, we were told, 'Leave it to the detectives,'" Wegener recalls. "But we felt certain that the grocery rapist lived in our neighborhood, and that we were more likely to catch a glimpse of him than the few detectives assigned to the case. The three known victims had provided the police with the rapist's description, and the detectives had an artist's conception, but incredibly, no one would give us a copy! I called the chief and said, 'This is silly. Give us the drawing!' He refused. I called all over the department, and no one would talk to me. Finally, a community relations officer gave me a copy of the sketch. Almost overnight, we distributed a thousand around the neighborhood."

After the assault on Wegener's neighbor, the grocery rapist's attacks stopped. "The word-of-mouth about the organizing apparently convinced him to lay low." But not low enough. A few weeks after the police sketch was distributed, a local woman spotted him, followed him home, and called the police with his address. The grocery rapist turned out to be a young loner in his twenties who lived three blocks from the Wegeners.

"BLOCK WALKS" AND SHRIEK ALARMS

West Philadelphia also pioneered the modern-day community patrol. "We didn't even use the term 'patrol,' " Wegener says. "It sounded too much like the police. We were unarmed and we didn't want to create any impression that we were vigilantes. We called them 'block walks.' The idea was simply to encourage people to get out of their homes and walk around the neighborhood together at night. We had groups of people tour the area for a few hours several times a week." Neighborhood surveillance was part of the idea, but given the minimal patrol time, it played a minor role. The real emphasis was on furthering neighborhood friendships, and on encouraging people to "take back the night."

The block walks, however, had a problem—communication. "We needed a way for the walkers—really anyone in the neighborhood—to signal for help. We needed a recognizable sound to alert people to investigate and call the police. We rejected whistles because they didn't sound urgent enough, and because some of the older people had trouble with them. Then someone suggested the freon horns used at football games. Their sound was instantly recognizable, very piercing, and you didn't need strong lungs to use them. They were a big hit right away." West Philadelphia's freon horns evolved into today's shriek alarms.

As the work progressed, crime in West Philadelphia declined. The grocery rapist was no longer a threat, the streets felt less mean, and neighbors became friendlier. Many people target-hardened their homes and installed windowsill flower boxes. ("Our ex-burglar told us they help prevent break-ins.") Teens and the elderly were integrated into the program, and tensions between the "older" and "younger" generations decreased, along with two of their frequent expressions, vandalism and harassment. Of course, crime did not disappear. It never does. What disappeared was the gnawing dread of "crime out of control." That dread was replaced by feelings of confidence in local mutual aid, which prevented many crimes and provided perspective on those that did occur—one crime in particular.

"NO 'KITTY GENOVESE' HERE"

Toward the end of 1975, Susan Speeth, a thirty-seven-year-old laboratory assistant, moved to one of West Philadelphia's organized blocks. A recent arrival, she did not know the city well and her new neighborhood hardly at all. Speeth was also recently divorced and in the midst of a difficult emotional adjustment. The people in her building tried to interest her in the block organization, but she was too preoccupied to care. She just wanted to be left alone. Nonetheless, her neighbors tried to introduce her to the hazards of the area. Despite the successful organizing effort, street assault was still a problem, especially for women out alone at night.

At 8 P.M. on October 3, Susan Speeth left her apartment and walked up South 48th Street. A young man appeared and brandished a knife, apparently intending to rob her. She screamed, and he stabbed her.

At Speeth's first scream, several neighbors rushed out of their homes. Others called the police, who arrived quickly. Two of the first to reach the fallen woman were a doctor and nurse. They tried to revive her but it was too late.

The killing caused a media sensation: "Woman Murdered in Area Famed for Crime Prevention." The stabbing was, of course, a tragedy, and it served as a grim reminder that even successful neighborhood programs do not completely eradicate crime. But the reaction in West Philadelphia to the murder of Susan Speeth was completely different from the reaction in Kew Gardens to the killing of Kitty Genovese. Most of those who heard Genovese's cries retreated deeper into fear and isolation, but the West Philadelphians immediately organized more than a hundred neighbors into a candlelight vigil, in Wegener's words, to "help nip any panic in the bud." After the Genovese murder, the residents of Kew Gardens felt ashamed. In West Philadelphia, however, no one felt that way. Instead, they reaffirmed their commitment to the organizing effort. They were outraged by the killing, but drew some comfort from their neighbors' quick responses.

In New York, several psychologists said the disregard for Genovese's cries was a "sign of the times," a result of "urban depersonalization." In West Philadelphia, however, there was no such hand-wringing. By the time of the Speeth killing, the residents had been dealing with the local crime situation for four years. They recognized that it was an isolated incident. There were no invocations of the "concrete jungle," no lame excuses for not getting involved. The West Philadelphians reacted not with rationalizations but with *analysis.*

They knew the victim. She was a recent arrival unfamiliar with the area, and preoccupied with personal problems. She ignored her neighbors' warnings about street crime, and presumably, was not paying attention that night. As a result, the assault quickly reached the altercation stage, when the best response is to hand over the money as calmly and quietly as possible. Instead, Speeth screamed, apparently unnerving her assailant, and he stabbed her.

No one *blamed* Susan Speeth for her death. It was impossible to know whether she would have survived if she hadn't screamed, and in a better world, knife-wielding robbers would not prowl the streets. But neither did the West Philadelphians panic over their own safety. To the extent that the victim was an actor in the tragic drama that resulted in her death, other residents knew they could act differently and probably avoid a similar fate.

Finally, Kitty Genovese's murderer was caught by a lucky accident. A milkman happened to notice Winston Moseley near the scene and identified him. Today there are no milkmen. If that killing had occurred a few years later, Moseley probably would have escaped; he *did escape* after three previous rape-murders he later admitted. Susan Speeth's killer, on the other hand, was captured *because of* the block-organizing effort. Neighbors saw a young man flee on foot, suggesting that he lived nearby. After four years of working together, they had a sense of the local young men who fit the assailant's description, who might be capable of such a thing. Suspicions centered on a particularly troubled young man who lived nearby. A neighbor spoke with his mother. She confronted him. He confessed, and his mother called the police.

"The Kitty Genovese example comes up all the time," Ellie Wegener says. "A street killing can happen in any community. The real question is, are people prepared to deal with that possibility? When a community has developed a good mutual support system, it's as ready as it can be. When there's no support, no community spirit, then all you have is a group of strangers like the neighbors who refused to help Kitty Genovese. But it doesn't have to be that way. When people take responsibility for the security of their own neighborhood, the crime rate drops, and people feel proud of what they've accomplished. Then, if something happens, they're ready and they respond."

GRANDPARENTS WITH WALKIE-TALKIES

The Dimond district of Oakland, California, is a largely white, middle-class neighborhood near largely black, lower-income East Oakland. With its substantial elderly population, it attracted street assailants for many years. Muggings and purse-snatchings were common. Many residents tried not to go out alone, even during the day. Those who did avoided Dimond Park, a hangout for drunks and drug addicts and a high-risk area for assault.

But one local resident refused to be intimidated. Hazel Manica, a sixty-eight-year-old grandmother, said she "just got sick of seeing people beaten up." Manica herself was no stranger to crime. Twice she'd been threatened with robbery, once by "scary motorcycle-gang types." Both times, she refused to assume the victim role. She screamed at her assailants to leave her alone, and they did. But she had many friends who had not been so fortunate.

In 1980, Manica organized twenty-five friends and neighbors, aged fifty to eighty-one (most over sixty-five), into the Dimond Community Safety Patrol (DCSP). Armed with walkie-talkies and bright yellow jackets, the mostly elderly crime fighters stroll their neighborhood in teams of two for several hours every afternoon. If they spot anything suspicious, they radio their dispatcher, who calls the police. "The police come quick when we call," Manica says. "We've helped them a lot. We're their eyes and ears out here." Since the DCSP began strolling the streets, parks, and shopping areas of the Dimond district, crime in the neighborhood has declined 48 percent.

For one crime, however, DCSP volunteers intervene differently. The crime is juvenile shoplifting, and the response is a tough scolding. The DCSP patrols the aisles of local stores where shoplifting has long been a problem. The situation was a major concern to the area's merchants, but there seemed to be no constructive way to deal with it. Signs warning that shoplifters would be prosecuted had little effect on the twelve- and thirteen-year-old thieves. The merchants were reluctant to saddle local kids with police records simply for stealing candy bars, but they felt they had no alternative. When they did turn someone in, however, the juvenile authorities simply released the child into parental custody. The kids were often back in the stores the next day, emboldened by the lack of punishment. Some community residents resented the merchants for taking such a hard line, while others shared their bitterness at the courts for releasing the shoplifters without punishment.

Enter the DCSP. When Manica sees a shoplifting, she marches up to the young offender and grabs him or her by the wrist: "I scold them like a grandmother. 'Put that back!' I say, 'I saw you take it! Don't you know right from wrong? You ought to be ashamed of yourself!' " The kids are not only ashamed, they're astonished. It's not clear whether the rate of shoplifting has declined, but throughout the neighborhood the kids all recognize "the old-lady cops," and area merchants are big DCSP supporters. So are many others. Recently, a nearby area organized a CSP of its own, and the Oakland-based Kaiser Corporation provided the funds for the group's jackets and walkie-talkies.

The scolding tactic also helped reclaim Dimond Park from, in Manica's words, "the drunks and dopers." Joseph Perillo, a gardener at the park, says he'd "tried everything from conciliation to calling the police to get the derelicts out, but nothing worked." However, a city employee's bureaucratic authority is apparently no match for an assertive elderly person's moral authority. After the DCSP launched a relentless scolding and shaming campaign, the winos and junkies stopped congregating in the park, at least during the day. "They've improved things 1,000 percent," Perillo says.

Matt Peskin, executive director of the National Association of Town Watch, estimates that 5 million Americans in 20,000 communities have become involved in community patrols. Some walk; others use automobiles. Some patrol during the day; others work at night. The participants range in age from teens to the elderly. Successful patrols work in coordination with local police. Many receive training in observation and reporting skills. Most are equipped with walkie-talkies or CB radios, but do not carry weapons or apprehend suspects. For information on starting a patrol in your area, contact your local police crime-prevention unit or the organizations listed in Resources.

THE GUARDIAN ANGELS CONTROVERSY

Community patrols work best in the context of a comprehensive neighborhood organizing effort, but even without block organizing, the DCSP's experience suggests that patrols by themselves can help control crime, in part because their visibility deters would-be wrongdoers, and in part because the DCSP volunteers are mostly senior citizens. Street assailants often see the elderly as attractive targets, but the sight of older people asserting themselves against crime apparently unnerves them enough to have a deterrent effect.

The DCSP's "grandparents" image has also defused another problem intrinsic to civilian parapolice efforts, charges of "vigilantism," or being "a crime-prone gang." Such charges have made at least one civilian street patrol, the Guardian Angels, the focus of considerable controversy.

The Guardian Angels are unarmed volunteers who patrol the New York City subway system. The young men and women, mostly in their teens and twenties, all wear red berets and T-shirts with red insignia. Since their founding in 1979, the Angels have grown from a band of thirteen to more than five hundred in New York alone, with chapters in a dozen cities. They have attracted a good deal of publicity, largely because of the charisma of their founder, Curtis Sliwa.

It's impossible not to applaud the Guardian Angels' goals: to help subway riders feel safer; to provide positive role models for underprivileged youth; and to gain the personal satisfaction that comes from belonging to a force for good. It's also difficult to argue with their recruitment requirements: a full-time job (or enrollment in school) and no arrest record. But the Guardian Angels have made almost as many enemies as friends in their short, high-profile history. Several cities, notably Detroit, with its model crime-prevention program, have been openly hostile to them. Some of the controversy is tinged with racial prejudice. Many Angels are young, tough, and nonwhite, the stereotype of the street assailants many people fear. But the more substantive criticism is that the Guardian Angels are "carpetbaggers."

"My problem with them," Detroit Police Chief Hart says, "is their lack of accountability. I have nothing against civilian patrols; we have several. We also have one thousand junior police cadets, teens who provide escort services for seniors in some of our public housing projects. But they're local people who live in the neighborhoods where they work. They're trained by and responsible to police officers, who are accountable to the city. The Angels come from far away saying they're going to 'clean up Detroit.' They take their orders from Mr. Sliwa in New York. I guess they haven't heard about the strides we've made in getting our crime problem under control."

Faced with similar objections elsewhere, including New York, Sliwa has countered that working too closely with police would compromise the group's effectiveness because the police and their auxiliaries are not trusted in many neighborhoods where the Angels live and patrol. In New York, after lengthy negotiations with city officials, the Angels have been accorded semiofficial status as an autonomous citizens group unaffiliated with the police. But they have agreed to work with a police liaison officer and wear city-issued registration badges to prevent "counterfeit Angels" from using the group's uniform as a cover for crime. In exchange, they get free subway passes. (Official relations vary from city to city where the Angels operate.) But the controversy surrounding the Guardian Angels is unlikely to subside as long as their accountability problem remains.

Community patrols can help deter street crime, and groups like the Angels represent welcome role models for young people who might otherwise yield to impulse and opportunity. But in the final analysis, security can't be "delivered" by any police agency, whether formal or informal. Policing is certainly necessary, but police can do little unless neighborhood residents take responsibility for their own safety. The best civilian patrols are incorporated into comprehensive crime-prevention efforts, where residents know patrollers by name, as neighbors. More anonymous patrols like the Guardian Angels may help people feel safer in the no-man's-land of the New York subway system, but for community patrols to be accountable to those they serve, they should develop indigenously, work closely with local police, and limit their activities to the neighborhoods where they live.

THE ELEMENTS OF SUCCESSFUL PROGRAMS

• *Keep things small.* Crime-prevention projects depend on transforming "strangers" into "neighbors," replacing anonymity with first-name acquaintanceships. Group size is a crucial factor. That's why many successful programs use block groups as their fundamental unit. In areas with apartment houses, organizing by floor or building might be more appropriate. In rural areas, other boundaries can define workable areas. There is no "right" number of participants, but when in doubt, keep things small.

• *Be patient and persistent.* Don't be disappointed if only a few neighbors show interest at first. Most people lead busy lives, and given the pervasive myth that "nothing works against crime," it takes time to become persuaded that personal involvement *can* make a difference. In the event of a local crime crisis, however, another problem arises—transitory interest. When a rapist is on the loose, people often become deeply involved, then lose interest after the criminal has been caught. One way to minimize this is to broaden the focus from merely "fighting crime" to "building a better neighborhood" through involvement in noncrime concerns. Finally, try not to write off people who decline to participate. As the group gains momentum, new members will seek it out, *if* they feel welcome.

• *Make friends. Have fun.* No need to be grim about crime prevention. Successful programs mix business and pleasure and often emphasize the latter. Friendship is the glue of community cohesion. Keep meetings informal. Meet in someone's home. Serve refreshments. Include people of all ages. Take some time to get to know each other.

• *Develop a phone list.* Draw an informal map of the organizing unit and distribute lists of names, addresses, and phone numbers. Include the names of all young people. Being "on the map" helps develop a feeling of belonging, especially for teens. It also saves time in the event of trouble. Update the list as people move and present a copy to new neighbors to welcome them into the neighborhood— and the group.

• *Survey members' skills.* Most groups are surprised to learn how much their members have to offer. Appreciating members' skills help them feel valued, and enhances community cohesion.

• *Be sensitive to ethnic and generational issues.* The group should reflect the racial, ethnic, and age composition of the block. One way to foster interethnic cooperation is to share ethnic foods at meetings. Be sure to reach out to older people and teens. The former are often good block-watchers; retirees may be home with time to spare. The latter need recognition for pro-social activities. Some innovative programs have placed older people in supervisory roles over teens who earn money by trimming shrubbery, helping with target-hardening, or providing senior escort services.

• *Involve your local crime-prevention unit, but guard against overdependence on the police.* Invite crime-prevention officers to your meetings. They'll be interested to learn what you're doing, and should be able to provide assistance with security surveys, Operation Identification, and "intelligence" about the crime situation in your area. But overreliance on the police should be carefully avoided. It discourages neighborhood residents from taking responsibility for their own safety. When community-based programs have failed— and many have—the typical reason has been that the residents continued to expect the police to "deliver" a safer community. Work closely with the police, but make sure your members see them as consultants, not as saviors.

• *Use existing community organizations.* No need to reinvent the wheel. Many communities already have organizations that can provide help, resources, and possibly even small grants.

• *Use the media.* Let local reporters and editors know about your work. You're news, and your group undoubtedly has important things to say. Media coverage gives a tremendous boost to group morale. It's an excellent recruitment vehicle, and it advertises community preparedness to criminals.

• *Give awards.* Volunteers need recognition for work well done. Awards dinners are a great way to honor key participants. Block club T-shirts or decals also help build neighborhood cohesion; they're especially popular with young people.

• *Erect Neighborhood Watch signs.* Some communities use "Warning" signs. Others project a more positive message: "Welcome to this Neighborhood Watch community."

• *Develop a neighborhood crime map.* Periodic maps pinpointing local crime incidents are well worth the effort. They locate crimes specifically, keep rumors under control, and allow residents to chart their progress toward a safer community.

• *Compile a victimization survey.* Just when a neighborhood begins to feel safer, the police sometimes report a huge *increase* in the area's crime rate. The typical reason is that the organizing effort has improved police-community relations to the point where residents report crimes that previously would have gone unreported. One way around this is to conduct informal victimization surveys of your own. There's no need for anything elaborate. A simple one-page handout can survey residents' victimization experiences during the previous six or twelve months. Ideally, the first survey should be conducted before any real crime-prevention work begins. The combination of police statistics, a neighborhood crime map, and victimization surveys should provide a reasonable picture of the crime situation in your community.

For more information about organizing a neighborhood crime-prevention group, see Resources.

DEFENSIBLE SPACE: CRIME PREVENTION
BY DESIGN

Community cohesion involves more than simply the organizational skills of a neighborhood's residents. The buildings can either attract antisocial activity or dissuade it. In 1973, Oscar Newman, a professor of City Planning at New York University, published *Defensible Space: Crime Prevention Through Urban Design,* which argues that the size and arrangement of buildings and open spaces, indoors and out, can substantially reduce opportunities for crime by subtly encouraging a sense of community among residents.

The concept of defensible space emerged, as many new ideas do, from an unexpected inconsistency. In 1969, Newman noticed that the Van Dyke housing project in Brooklyn, New York, had twice as much crime as the Brownsville project. What piqued Newman's curiosity was that the two developments were located across the street from one another, and their populations were almost identical. Both had the same racial and ethnic compositions, average family size, average income and percentage on welfare. They also had the same total acreage, number of buildings, and population density. But the higher-crime Van Dyke development was composed almost entirely of fourteen-story buildings, while the lower-crime Brownsville project was a mixture of three- and six-story buildings in more of a "village" arrangement:

The high-rise apartment tower is [one] real villain. Larger buildings encourage crime by fostering feelings of anonymity, isolation, irresponsibility, and lack of identification with surroundings. [In one year] total felonies for all [New York City] housing projects varied from 8.8 per 1,000 in three-story buildings to 20.2 per 1,000 in buildings of 16 stories or more.

Another design aspect critical to crime is the arrangement of units sharing a common hall. High crime rates persist when every apartment on a floor opens onto the same hall (a "double-loaded" corridor). But when five or fewer apartments open onto semiprivate courtyard-style foyers, the crime rate drops by as much as 50 percent. "In a high-rise apartment with double-loaded corridors, the only defensible spaces are the interiors of the apartments themselves; everything else is 'no-man's land.' Sparsely used and impossible to survey, these areas become a nether world of fear and crime." The courtyard approach, on the other hand, fosters face-to-face relations among those who share the common space. It decreases anonymity and isolation and encourages informal surveillance and identification with other residents on the floor.

Newman's work, and other researchers' experiments with his concepts (several of which have been incorporated into 7-Eleven's robbery-prevention program) demonstrate that "deopportunizing crime" can—and should—be designed into new housing developments and shopping areas. Of course, most of us have no input into the design of our neighborhoods; we move into areas built years before our arrival. But defensible-space concepts can be used to *modify* existing blocks, and even when that's not possible, Newman's insights can help analyze a neighborhood and locate potential trouble spots.

In 1971 in the notoriously high-crime Bedford-Stuyvesant neighborhood of Brooklyn, one block was modified using Newman's concepts. The street was closed to through traffic and symbolic portals were constructed at each end of the block. A playground was built in the midblock area, flanked by angled parking for residents. Benches were placed nearby. Less than two years later "residents said that street assaults had been almost eliminated, that homes were burglarized less frequently, and that drug addicts noticeably avoided the area."

Not surprisingly, such modifications contribute to the success of other crime-prevention efforts. In 1974, Hartford, Connecticut, introduced block organizing to two adjacent neighborhoods, North and South Asylum Hill. Then physical modifications were made in the north area only: Several through streets were changed to cul-de-sacs, symbolic portals were erected at entrances, and the area was re-landscaped to increase feelings of local territoriality. In the modified area, crime dropped by one-third compared to the unmodified area.

HOW TO REDUCE VANDALISM UP TO 75 PERCENT

Missing street signs, razor-slashed bus seats, graffiti. Vandalism has been called "America's premiere folk crime." Vandalism is not "serious enough" to be an index crime, but it costs Americans $1 billion a year, far more than armed robbery. It also takes an enormous aesthetic toll on the environment.

Most people, including police, throw up their hands in frustration at vandalism, but vandalism-prevention expert James Wise has shown that simple steps can reduce it by up to 75 percent. Wise, a professor of architecture at the University of Washington, writes that most vandalism is not random mischief. Like most other crimes, it's opportunistic. Wise writes that common-sense preventive efforts are the key to vandalism control:

Easy targets are the most likely to be vandalized. In a park near Seattle, light fixtures that overhung a path were broken repeatedly. The path led to a baseball diamond, and the glass globes were just within bat reach of exuberant, or dejected, players on their way home. Rotating the globes upwards 180 degrees put them out of reach, and stopped the breakage. In a recent survey of vandalism at outdoor recreation facilities, 80 percent of stolen or user-damaged items were within reach of 95 percent of passers-by.

In addition to the easy target, the *visibility damaged target* attracts abuse. In a famous experiment, Stanford University psychologist Philip Zimbardo abandoned two cars, hoods up, without license plates, one in a poor part of the Bronx, New York, the other in upper-middle-class Palo Alto, California:

The car in the Bronx was attacked within 10 minutes, first by a family—father, mother, and young son—who removed the radiator and battery. Within 24 hours, virtually everything of value had been removed. Then random destruction began. Windows were smashed, parts torn off, upholstery ripped. Children began to use what remained as a playground.

The car in Palo Alto remained untouched for weeks. Then Zimbardo smashed part of it with a sledgehammer. Soon, passers-by joined in. Within hours, the car had been turned upside down and utterly destroyed.

Untended property becomes fair game for people out for fun or plunder, even for those who ordinarily would not dream of doing such things. Because of the nature of community life in the Bronx—its anonymity, past experiences of "no one caring," and the frequency with which vehicles are abandoned—the vandalism began more quickly than in Palo Alto, where possessions are more cared for. Vandalism occurs once communal barriers are lowered by actions that signal that "no one cares."

Wise writes that most vandalism is aided by the physical characteristics of the target itself. As a result, design can be used to steer people away from defacement and destruction. He emphasizes the necessity to "deopportunize design" by building protective features into public facilities, while at the same time welcoming users: "Placing benches at the intersections of paths or street corners discourages 'corner cutting' over delicate landscapes. Benches are better than fences; both impede passage, but the former add a friendly note by providing a place to rest."

Deopportunizing design also extends to reducing vandalism's "sensory rewards." Metal roadsigns are frequent shooting targets in rural areas because they make such a resounding "clang" when hit. Plywood signs make a less satisfying sound, and attract less target practice. Similarly, large plate glass windows shatter more dramatically than smaller windows. Window breaking can be reduced by using small panes.

HOW TO CONTROL GRAFFITI

Graffiti, one of the most ubiquitous forms of vandalism, is also one of the oldest. The Pharaohs tried unsuccessfully to prevent laborers from carving personal marks into the Pyramids, and Nebuchadnezzar railed against graffiti on the temples of Babylonia.

The ancient kings could have taken a lesson from Kathy Hoard of the Crary/St. Mary's neighborhood. Even after the Neighborhood Watch program cut the area's crime rate in half, fear of crime remained high, especially among older residents. To some extent, this was to be expected: Fear lingers long after statistics change. But when Hoard asked her elderly neighbors *why* they still felt afraid, most mentioned the gang- and violence-oriented graffiti all over the neighborhood. Hoard sympathized: "I couldn't stand it either. The graffiti made my blood boil."

Hoard mentioned her concern at a community council meeting, and despite the skepticism of fellow members, volunteered to organize a graffiti-removal campaign. With the support of local crime-prevention officer Nelson Scheuer, she surveyed the neighborhood in early 1981, and mapped more than 150 graffiti sites. Then she spent several months securing the owners' permission to repaint their defaced walls. "Many," she recalls, "were very pessimistic. Some had already repainted several times." That summer, Hoard recruited local residents to paint over the graffiti. Many teens participated. Like Tom Sawyer's fence painters, they enjoyed painting publicly visible walls. Several later admitted painting some of the graffiti. But under Hoard's direction, refacing the community offered more rewards than defacing it. Participants not only had fun, they also received "Spirit of Detroit" community service awards at a gala postcampaign banquet. And because their efforts had given them a stake in graffiti-free walls, they helped keep the problem to a minimum by influencing their peers not to paint graffiti. After two years, only two new graffiti incidents occurred in the 156-block neighborhood. They were quickly painted over.

NEIGHBORHOOD-BASED CONFLICT RESOLUTION

This incident might happen anywhere: Two next-door neighbors, both quiet, hard-working family men, who have quarreled repeatedly about rights to the parking place between their two driveways, get into another argument. But this time something snaps and one winds up shooting the other. The media call the incident "senseless violence." Those who hear about it sigh, "The world is full of crazies . . ." On the block where it happened, the residents feel terribly upset: "How could something like *that* happen *here?* This is a good street, a quiet street, with nice homes, good people."

At first glance such violence may seem "crazy" or "irrational." It's certainly tragic, but rarely senseless. Most violence between people who know one another is the culmination of years of increasingly acrimonious arguments, marked by a chronic breakdown of communication.

If this dispute had occurred in any of nineteen San Francisco neighborhoods, the outcome might have been different. San Francisco is the home of the Community Boards Program, a volunteer-based, conflict-resolution effort that trains local residents to mediate disputes in their own backyards. I've been a member for several years, and the experience has been profound.

Most neighborhood conflicts occupy a gray area between "non-crime" and "crime," with the former often escalating into the latter over time, as in the case of the parking argument that leads to a shooting. Noncrimes are often as infuriating as crimes. They're just not as clearly against the law: noise problems from barking dogs, loud music, or home workshops; youth problems involving mischief, harassment, or loitering; and the myriad other differences of opinion that inevitably arise when people live in close proximity. These are the problems Community Boards members handle through a process that encourages disputants to bring their problems before nonjudicial panels of their neighbors. During the program's eight-year history, it has held hundreds of panel hearings, more than 80 percent of which have resulted in mutually signed, usually lasting resolutions.

The Community Boards concept developed in 1975 when Raymond Shonholtz, a former trial attorney, became intrigued with programs in Norway, Scotland, and Seattle that used citizen panels to deal with juvenile delinquency and other problems. While exploring the citizens-panel concept, he came to see the problems of the court system in a new light:

> The myth is that the courts are overburdened. In fact, they are misused. Few cases require complex, formal court procedures, but because no other conflict-resolution forum exists, people with a dispute must choose between using the courts or tolerating the problem. Few people choose the courts willingly. (Every) court is quite literally "the court of last resort."
> Why? Because courts are insensitive. They impose unnecessary formality. There is a sense of futility in court. When people weigh the possible return against the real time, money, and social costs, many are discouraged from using the courts at all.
> The public generally views the justice system as ineffective. It delivers neither appropriate restitution nor appropriate punishment. Low-income people generally mistrust the justice system and cannot afford it. More affluent people prefer alternatives to it. The result is that many victims and witnesses refuse to participate in their own cases, which translates to case dismissals and plea bargains on the criminal side, and defaults and compromises on the civil side.

In Shonholtz's view, this situation has many negative results:

• The problems inherent in the court system discourage early conflict resolution and force individuals and communities to tolerate festering disputes until they become urgent, that is, "crimes."

• The justice system undermines neighbors' feelings of responsibility for those around them, and compromises their self-respect. Neighborhood people are often aware of youth problems and wife and child abuse, but because of the criminal justice system's tendency either to do nothing or to overreact, no one calls the police until the situation becomes unbearable. The police find a full-blown crisis and criticize the neighbors for "apathy." The neighbors feel guilty about waiting as long as they did, and their self-respect suffers. But what could they have done? Although they could see the problem developing, until it became a "crime," it was a noncrime, and everyone knows the police don't do anything about noncrimes.

• The courts *promote* crime. Because misuse of the system has generated such an enormous case load, only "serious" crimes receive genuine attention. The youth who shoplifts is almost never held accountable for his or her misconduct. Without accountability the misbehavior appears permissible, and the frequent lack of response, beyond a slap on the wrist, does little to discourage continued wrongdoing.

• The court system suppresses the real conflict. By the time a dispute has its day in court, the factors that generated it often appear insignificant compared to the act on trial.

• Courts encourage dishonesty. By assigning "guilt" rather than encouraging all parties to take responsibility for their part in the dispute, the judicial process invites those involved to manipulate the conflict for fear that honesty will achieve a less favorable result.

• The criminal justice system compromises the authority of the family. Parents are, of course, reluctant to see their children in jeopardy. Even when they know their child has done wrong, they are placed in the position of having to offer comfort in the hostile court environment, instead of clearly disapproving of their child's behavior.

Shonholtz concluded that most people involved with the court system in any capacity other than attorney or judge emerge as losers. Victims receive neither restitution nor satisfaction. Offenders are either ignored and dismissed, or turned into "examples" and "put away." They get no constructive help to resolve the conflicts in which they participated. Finally, because disputes are rarely resolved, just suppressed, they inevitably reemerge, and society as a whole pays the price.

In 1977, with the help of a few veteran community organizers and a core group of volunteers in one San Francisco neighborhood, Shonholtz developed the Community Boards model of neighborhood conciliation. The goal was simple: To enable neighbors to help each other resolve disputes at no cost to any party, without lawyers or formal court procedures, and to encourage all parties to take responsibility for their actions.

Coordinated by a central office that handles policy, fund-raising, and training, the Community Boards Program maintains six largely autonomous offices around San Francisco that handle disputes in participating neighborhoods. When a case comes in—either brought directly by a disputant or referred by another agency—a "case developer" visits those involved and assesses their willingness to meet with a Community Boards panel. If the disputants are willing (about one-third are), several panelists are enlisted to hear the case. Panel members, all trained in conflict resolution, come from the disputants' neighborhood. Care is taken to select panelists similar to the disputants in race, ethnic, and age characteristics. Bilingual and teen panelists are recruited when necessary.

At the hearing, often held at a neighborhood church, the disputants present their versions of the problem, and outline the resolution each thinks would be fair to all concerned. Panel members neither judge nor cross-examine. Instead, they listen. They question the parties, not to trick them into contradicting themselves, as attorneys would, but rather to make sure they have expressed all their concerns. The panelists let the disputants know that they cannot resolve the conflict "for" them; the parties must do that for themselves. In more than 80 percent of panel hearings, the disputants negotiate a mutually acceptable resolution within four hours. The panel then drafts an agreement that outlines what each party has agreed to do. Each disputant signs the agreement and keeps a copy for reference. One panel member volunteers to follow the case to see how the resolution works out and, if necessary, to reconvene the panel. Disputants are often so pleased with the process, they frequently inquire about the next Community Boards training program so they can sit on panels themselves.

The Community Boards process, like so much of crime prevention, is a mixture of the mundane and the near-miraculous. I've been a panelist on cases where the parties arrived at the hearing seemingly unwilling to compromise, threatening to sue each other, and at times on the brink of violence. But four hours later, at the signing of the resolution, they're transformed. They feel they've been heard and taken seriously. Their dispute has been resolved to their mutual satisfaction, and their shattered relationship has been restored or is on the mend.

The Community Boards Program has been credited with helping to head off a gang war at San Francisco's Woodrow Wilson High School. Tensions between Filipino and Central American students had long been a problem. In 1980, a Hispanic student was shot to death at the school, and his friends blamed the Filipinos. The principal called Community Boards, and hearings were held to mediate fights, name-calling, and incidents of shoving on the cafeteria line.

Any of these might have exploded into gang violence, but with the help of Community Boards, they did not. Of course, the tensions have not disappeared; they probably never will. But they have not reached a flashpoint since the two sides began participating in the Community Boards process.

Community Boards has attracted interest from all over the country, and recently the program developed a manual to help other communities establish similar services.

The Community Boards Program is just one of a number of mediation services around the country that deal with neighborhood problems, landlord-tenant disputes, consumer complaints, and child custody and visitation arrangements. A recent evaluation by James Garofalo and Kevin Connelly, of the National Council on Crime and Delinquency, showed that mediation works quite well and at lower cost than the courts.

KITTY GENOVESE REVISITED

Austin Street in Kew Gardens hasn't changed much since Kitty Genovese was killed there twenty years ago, but many residents' attitudes toward crime have.

"Her death was a terrible thing," says fifty-seven-year-old Joseph Trommer, who has lived in Kew Gardens for much of his life, "but if the same thing happened here today, I think people would respond much differently." Trommer, a graduate engineer who works for a display-case manufacturing firm, ought to know. In 1981, he organized the Kew Gardens Civilian Patrol, initially hand-delivering flyers to six hundred homes. The two hundred-member patrol drives around the neighborhood from 6 P.M. to 2 A.M. every night, armed with communications equipment purchased with members' contributions and small grants from local businesses. The group coordinates its efforts with several block-watch groups, and has peppered the neighborhood with distinctive aluminum signs: "Warning! Area Patrolled by Trained Civilians in Marked and Unmarked Cars." The Kew Gardens organization is one of more than 135 neighborhood crime-prevention groups in New York City. The volunteers, who work one four-hour shift a month, radio for police assistance when necessary through their base station in a local senior citizens' home.

"This is a delightful neighborhood," Trommer says. "Of course, there's crime here, like everywhere, but about eight years ago, it became a crisis. The liquor and drug crowd began scaring people away from Forest Park. You'd hear glass breaking at all hours, and there were assaults and robberies. I'd been involved in the Kew Gardens Civic Association and we met with the police. They said they didn't have the manpower to patrol the area adequately. We realized that we were getting nowhere just complaining, so we got the patrol together to let the drug addicts and street criminals know that we weren't going to stand for them around here. At first, some of the police were skeptical; they saw us as a Mickey Mouse organization, but over the years, support has improved, and in the last three years, we've really turned Forest Park around. People take their kids there again. We persuaded some of the local merchants to stop selling beer in bottles. The drinkers still litter their beer cans, but there's not much broken glass anymore. The patrol has also prevented muggings and vandalism. Of course, you can't prevent every crime. Kew Gardens hasn't become Shangri-La. But it *is* safer."

What would people do if they heard a woman scream late at night? "I can't say that everyone would respond, but there would be much more response than there was to Kitty Genovese. There's more community awareness here now. We've had people stop purse-snatchings and assaults in the subway station here. I have a good alarm system in my home, and we have Operation Identification, but what good are they if you're afraid to walk out your front door? Crime is more than an individual concern; it's a community thing. My kids grew up playing in Forest Park. The kids here today should be able to do that, too. Sure, sometimes I wish the Civilian Patrol and the block watches weren't necessary. But they are and they work."

Resources:

"Community Crime Prevention and Neighborhood Organizing Packet"
by Ellie Wegener, National Crime Prevention Specialist
$5.00

Ellie Wegener
P.O. Box 1292
McLean, VA 22101

Wegener's packet is a potpourri of valuable tips for starting a block-based crime prevention program.

American Association of Retired Persons/
National Retired Teachers Association
George Sunderland, Coordinator, Crime Prevention Program
1909 K St. N.W.
Washington, DC 20049
(202) 872–4700

One of the oldest, largest crime-prevention programs in the country. Publishes many excellent resources.

The International Society of Crime Prevention Practitioners
1600 Research Blvd.
Rockville, MD 20850

A network that includes more than 800 U.S. crime-prevention police officers and community-based programs. An excellent source of information, training, referrals, and technical assistance.

The National Association of Town Watch
Matt A. Peskin, Executive Director
P.O. Box 769
Havertown, PA 19083
(251) 649–6662

Publishes a newsletter and provides technical assistance.

The National Rural Crime Prevention Center
See Resources, chapter 6

Defensible Space: Crime Prevention Through Urban Design
by Oscar Newman
1973, 425 pages
Collier/Macmillan Publishing Co.
866 Third Ave.
New York, NY 10022

"How to Organize a Graffiti-Removal Campaign"
by Kathy Hoard
1981, 26 pages, $10.00
Kathy Hoard
16175 Gilchrist
Detroit, MI 48235

The Community Boards Program
Raymond Shonholtz, Executive Director
149 Ninth St.
San Francisco, CA 94103
(415) 552-1250

Write or call for information about the materials the CBP has developed to help launch similar services around the country. Training and technical assistance are also available.

8

How to Support
the Recovery of a Crime Victim

MY MUGGING, PART 2

After I was robbed at gunpoint, my life took some strange turns. On one level I felt lucky. I'd escaped a life-threatening situation without physical injury. But on a deeper level I felt profoundly violated. I haven't been quite the same since.

When I got home that night, I felt numb. I'd always believed I had control over my life, but a gun pressed against your spine changes your assumptions about self-determination.

My wife and a few friends took care of me. They listened as I went over and over the assault. They tried to comfort me, but I could not be comforted. Someone offered to call the police, but I immediately vetoed the idea. Intellectually, I knew I should have called them, and today I regret not doing so. If the same thing happened to me again, I'd not only call the police but several key neighbors as well. At the time, however, I recoiled from reporting. I didn't mind telling my friends about the holdup; talking with them, it felt like recounting a bad dream. But if the police appeared, with all their questions, somehow I felt they would make the robbery "real," and I wasn't ready to face it. If an insurance claim had been involved, I would have called the police right away, as I did after our burglary. But my robbery loss was less than the deductible on my insurance, so there was no money in reporting it. Finally, I knew that the probability of the police catching my assailants was near zero. It was dark and everything had happened so quickly I didn't get a good enough look at them to describe them.

I may not have reported the robbery, but I definitely wanted my assailants punished—not sent to prison, but turned over to me for Old Testament retribution. I constructed elaborate revenge fantasies, but at the same time, felt upset about having them. I was confused and disoriented. I didn't trust myself.

Over the next few days, my life ran on automatic pilot. I went to work, did errands, saw friends. But I was just going through the motions. I felt angry and depressed.

In time, of course, my life returned to "normal." But normal felt different. Violent crime changes people. It's been ten years now, and I'm "over it," the way people get over any loss. You function, you laugh, you love; most days you don't think about it. But there's a little knot somewhere deep inside where there used to be none, and it aches every now and then.

THE STAGES OF GRIEVING AND RECOVERY

Reactions to crime vary, depending on the individual and the crime. Usually, the more violent the crime, the more difficult the recovery. Many victims of violent crime feel as though part of their personhood has died.

Immediately after rape, robbery, or assault, many victims experience shock, usually a contradictory combination of emotional outbursts and periods of withdrawal into numbness. Both reactions are normal. When they're able to discuss their feelings, victims often say, "I feel stunned"; "I'm like a zombie"; or "I can't feel anything." Disbelief and denial are also common. "I can't believe this happened to me."

Sometime after the initial shock—perhaps shortly after a theft, or up to several months after the murder of a loved one—victims begin to ask, "Why? Why did this happen to me?" At this stage (and possibly forever) the question has no answer, and victims may become angry at the entire universe. They may curse God as merciless, and lose their tempers with those who are trying to help. At the same time, they typically feel guilty about lashing out at their friends.

Next comes bargaining, the "if only" stage. As victims continue to ask why? they begin to take responsibility for what happened to them. I recall thinking, If only I hadn't turned down that street with the broken light. If only I'd seen what was coming. In my case, I *did* bear some responsibility, but bargaining takes place even when victims have nothing to do with the crime. The parents of a child murdered by a drunk driver might say, "If only we hadn't moved to this town. If only we were better parents . . ."

In time, bargaining changes to self-blame and anger turns inward; together they become depression. Victims may become distracted, suffer insomnia or sleep all the time, function poorly or not at all. They may become obsessed with their loss, but at the same time feel guilty and embarrassed about "dwelling on it." They often fear that their friends may consider them boring and self-pitying. They try to pick up the pieces of their lives, but for a time life seems meaningless. This stage can be particularly difficult for support people, because, depending on the violence of the crime, it may last quite a while.

Finally, the depression lifts and victims feel renewed energy. Sound judgment returns and preoccupation with the crime subsides. Acceptance, however, does not imply forgetting. Violent crime often scars victims for life.

The stages of grieving and recovery are neither distinct nor separate. They blend into each other, and depending on the crime and the victim's personality, the recovery process may vary. Victims may also experience "relapses" if the crime leads to a trial, sentencing, or parole hearing. These events force them to relive their experiences, and to some extent, recover from them all over again.

HOW TO HELP

Crime victims need three things: *support* from friends willing to listen throughout the grieving process; *permission* to recover in their own way; and the *power* to decide for themselves how to deal with the situation.

The more violent the crime, the more difficult it is to support recovery. The process takes time, and for a while the victim may act somewhat irrationally. Friends and family often find it difficult to understand that in the aftermath of violent crime, some irrationality is normal. These guidelines should help support people provide appropriate comfort:

• *Validate the victim's pain.* Support people should encourage victims to express their suffering fully. There's a natural tendency to say, "It's all right. It's over. Don't dwell on it." Such statements may be made with the best intentions, but from the victim's perspective, they're way off the mark. It's *not* all right. It's *not* over. The mourning process has only just begun. Don't dissuade victims from expressing their grief. They have every reason to feel upset. Sharing any tragedy may feel painful and awkward, but the best thing you can do is to *be there* for the victim.

• *Support the victim for surviving.* In violent assaults, most victims experience a wrenching fear of being killed. In this context, *anything the victim did to survive was the right thing to do.* Victims may torment themselves for "giving in," or being stupid. "I should have seen it coming." "I should have worn running shoes instead of high heels." "I should have fought more." The list of possible "should haves" is endless, and some victims are quite hard on themselves. Early in the grief process, friends should support victims for their resourcefulness. "You came through it. You survived." Suggestions about how to avoid future victimization should wait.

• *Listen. Really listen.* Don't deny the victim's feelings. Try to shape your comments to support what the victim says, even if you disagree. If a rape victim says, "My life is over," don't say, "Nonsense, you've got your whole life ahead of you." That may be true, but at that moment, the victim has every reason to believe that the life she knew before the assault *is* over. A more supportive statement would be, "It's natural to feel that way."

• *Some denial is normal.* If a violent-crime victim prefers not to talk, don't force conversation. The silence may feel oppressive, but some victims need to withdraw for a while. Others may affect a bizarre cheerfulness and launch into new projects as a way of denying their pain. Faced with such behavior, friends or family might worry that the victim isn't grieving "properly." If denial continues after several weeks (or months in the murder of someone close), such concern may be justified, but in the immediate aftermath, some denial is normal. If a victim withdraws into silence, a good way to communicate support without words is through touch. Gentle physical contact is a powerful healing force.

• *Don't give orders; ask questions.* Some people, especially men confronted with violence against a woman, pride themselves on being able to "take charge." This may seem helpful, but it does more harm than good. The victim has just been stripped of personal sovereignty. The support person's task is to help rebuild that precious sense of authority over self. Taking charge does not help restore self-determination; it merely subjects the victim to the will of yet another person, however well-intentioned. Don't say, "Lie down while I call the police." Instead, ask, "What do you want to do?" Put yourself at the victim's service: "I'll do anything you want. Just tell me what you need."

Law enforcement officials say every crime victim should call the police right away. This certainly makes sense. The police can't respond without a report. But in the immediate aftermath of victimization, be sensitive to the victim. If he or she would like to lie down or call a few friends before calling the police, support that.

When victims report crime experiences, the justice system sometimes compounds the dehumanization they already feel by viewing them as statistics, then relegating them to the minor role of witnesses while most of the attention shifts to the criminal: his rights, his problems, his lawyer, plea, and deal. Dealing with "the authorities" at a time when your own personal authority has just been shattered can be an ordeal. Despite improvements in police responses to rape and domestic violence, some victims still find officers unsympathetic. In such cases, reporting can be a nightmare. Again, be there for the victim. If the police behave inappropriately, let them—and their superiors—know how you feel they should respond.

• *Don't become the injured party.* Don't grab a gun and bound out of the house raving that you'll "get the animal who did this." Don't lose control of yourself. If you're not the victim, don't act as if you are. The *real* victim needs you to remain calm, rational, and responsive to his or her needs.

• *Keep listening.* Some victims repeat themselves. Some become terrible bores as they go over and over their feelings. Don't abandon them. Keep listening. Talking it out works. In 1980, the New York Victim Services Agency interviewed crime victims months after their victimizations. Those who did the most talking with the most support people reported the fewest lingering emotional problems.

• *Attend to your own needs for support.* Victimization can be a wrenching experience; so can supporting a victim. In the study just mentioned, the researchers also interviewed a victims' support people. One-third said the experience had made them feel "frightened, nervous, and less safe." It's important to recognize your own needs and, if necessary, to seek your own support. Otherwise, you may be unable to be there for your victimized friends.

RAISING THE ISSUE OF CRIME PREVENTION

• *If possible, don't raise the subject yourself.* Try to wait until the victim asks, "What could I have done differently?" Then don't answer; instead, turn the question around: "What do *you* think you could have done differently?" Give victims the opportunity to develop their own crime-prevention ideas, then either support them or reshape them based on the information in chapters 4 through 7. No one can "deliver" personal safety to anyone else. Each of us must take responsibility for our own well-being. The best way to teach is to equip people with resources that enable them to help themselves.

• *If you do raise the subject, wait for a "teachable moment."* If you offer advice before victims are ready to listen, they may be unable to take it in. Wait until you see signs of the acceptance stage: renewed energy and a return of laughter and sound judgment.

• *Direct a victim's thinking toward the future.* Victims often say they "should have known better"—and maybe they should have—but as they approach acceptance, support people should point them toward the future: "It's no use berating yourself with what you 'should have done.' What happened happened. The important thing is to concentrate on what you'd do differently in the future."

IF A WOMAN YOU LOVE GETS RAPED

To many men (and perhaps some women), "rape" simply connotes coerced sexual intercourse. This definition obscures the violence and degradation of this crime. Intercourse may have nothing to do with it. Rapists freely admit that the sexual aspect of rape is secondary to the desire to humiliate the victim. Sexual assault may be a crime of lust, but it's a lust for power, not necessarily for sex. For this reason, counselors prefer the term "sexual assault" to "rape." "Rape" focuses too much attention on the dimension of intercourse; "sexual assault" emphasizes the violence fundamental to this crime.

Authorities agree that sexual assault is the nation's number two violent crime, second only to wife beating. Despite increased police sensitivity, no more than 50 percent of sexual assaults are ever reported. Why the low reporting rate? Largely because many victims fear confrontations with police—and lovers—who may still believe the myths about this terrible violation:

• *She Was Asking For It.* This myth says that women who dress provocatively "invite" sexual assault. It makes as much sense as saying that men who wear expensive suits invite robbery. It fails to explain how nuns and grandmothers fall victim to this crime. There *is* an "invitation stage" to street assault, but it has to do with appearing distracted, not with "provocative" dress. A conservatively dressed woman in a fog is a more likely target of sexual assault than an alluringly dressed woman with an assertive stride and a look that says, "Don't mess with me."

• *You Can't Thread a Moving Needle.* This myth declares that rape is impossible because the victim must consent in order that the assailant be able to insert his penis into the opening of his choice. It makes as much sense as saying that mugging is impossible because the victim must consent to the transfer of funds for the robber to be able to remove his wallet. Weapons and death threats are the rule in rape, and attacks by groups are common. Most people become remarkably cooperative in the face of death threats by armed assailants who appear quite capable of murder. Finally, "threading the needle," that is, penetration, is not necessary for the victim to feel severely traumatized.

• *False Accusations.* "Rape," wrote the seventeenth-century English jurist Lord Chief Justice Matthew Hale, "is an accusation easily made and hard to prove." But how easy *is* it to make a false accusation of sexual assault? About as easy as accusing someone of a $100 mugging at gunpoint. A false accusation of mugging would be simple: The "victim" would not have to show any injury, only emotional distress, which is easy to fake. The "mugger" would not have to possess the money or any weapon for the crime to have taken place. In fact, it would be *easier* to make a false accusation of mugging than of rape because in the former, no one is interested in the victim's underwear or sexual history. If it's so easy to make false accusations of mugging, why don't more people make them? Because any such accusation invites police interrogation and life disruption, not to mention risk of prosecution if the accusation proves false. How many men would report a true case of anal rape, let alone a false accusation?

The guidelines for supporting recovery from sexual assault are similar to those mentioned earlier, with a few additions:

• *Police reporting.* If the victim chooses to report in hopes of getting a conviction, she should do so as quickly as possible, without changing clothes or bathing, which might destroy evidence. If she prefers to call a friend, change, bathe, then report, that's her prerogative, but it reduces the likelihood of conviction.

• *Medical help.* Don't rush the woman to an emergency room if she doesn't want to go. VD and pregnancy tests can wait. Support people should make medical decisions only if the victim is too injured to make them herself.

• *Rape crisis centers.* Many communities have rape counseling services. You might ask if the woman would like to call one.

• *Relationship counseling.* Sexual assault causes tremendous strains in even the most stable and supportive relationships. When the woman feels up to it, relationship counseling is usually a good idea.

• *Making love again.* This is the most difficult aspect of recovering from sexual assault. The woman may not want to make love for a while. Like all other decisions in the aftermath of rape, the decision to resume lovemaking should be left up to her.

Women's sexual reactions to rape vary considerably. Some want to make love right away to reassure themselves that their lovers still love them, don't blame them, and don't consider them "soiled." Others cannot even think of sex for a long time. One woman might want to be held and cuddled immediately, but may need time before she feels comfortable with sexuality. Another might get angry and remind her lover of the times he may have crossed the line from coaxing to coercion. While exercising patience, however, a man should reassure a lover recovering from sexual assault that he still loves her and still wants to make love with her.

Recovery from any assault is difficult. Recovery from sexual assault is more so. For a man, helping a lover recover from rape takes time, love, and patience. Professional counseling for both lovers is usually a good idea.

VICTIM ASSISTANCE PROGRAMS

The concept of reparations to crime victims is as old as civilization itself. More than 3,500 years ago, the code of Hammurabi required Babylonian thieves to make restitution. Later, victim restitution was incorporated into penal law, with the last share of payment going to the state. In Old French, this share was called the *fin*, hence our word, "fine." By the eighteenth century, legal theorists had come to view all crimes as offenses against the state, not against the victims. This perspective was progressive to the extent that it curtailed personal revenge and helped solidify the legal system. But it also "robbed" victims of compensation for their injuries and losses. Recently, concern for crime victims has increased markedly. The 1982 President's Task Force on Victims of Crime recommended that victims be heard at every step of the justice process, from bail hearings to parole reviews, a right already granted in Arizona, California, and Connecticut.

Today more than thirty states have Victim Assistance Programs (VAPs) that award up to $45,000 to victims depending on their injuries, rehabilitative needs, and work time lost. VAPs vary, but most limit support to victims of violent crimes. The typical VAP requires reporting within forty-eight hours and documentation of lost income and medical and rehabilitation expenses. Unfortunately, only a small proportion of eligible victims ever file VAP claims, largely because the programs are not well publicized. For information, contact your local district attorney's office, or the National Organization for Victim Assistance.

INCOME TAX RELIEF FOR CRIME LOSSES

If you itemize your deductions on Schedule A, financial losses from crime and other disasters not covered by insurance may be deducted on your federal income tax return. You must be able to prove that a theft loss did, in fact, occur; the best way is to attach a copy of the police report. Theft losses are subject to a $100 deductible, and limited to their purchase price or fair market value, whichever is *less*. Figure your theft-loss deduction on IRS Form 4684, "Casualties and Thefts," then enter the net loss on line 24 of Schedule A.

Tax regulations change. For current information, contact your local IRS office and ask for Publication #547, "Tax Information on Disasters, Casualties and Thefts."

BEYOND RECOVERY

Psychologists say the recovery process ends with "acceptance," when victims have processed their grief and reconstructed their lives. There is, however, another stage beyond acceptance—action. Crime victims can become key people in neighborhood crime-prevention efforts. They know only too well what victimization means, and recounting their experiences can make crime real for neighbors who might otherwise not be interested in building community cohesiveness.

Action also hastens recovery. It helps derive meaning from victimization experiences and encourages people to see themselves not just as "victims," but as crime-fighters in a unique position to lead their neighbors in important work. Grieving and recovery are important, and victims should be encouraged to take all the time they need. But beyond recovery, victims can play an important role in building safer communities. Don't just mourn; organize.

Resource:

National Organization for Victim Assistance (NOVA)
700 North Fairfax St., Suite 260
Alexandria, VA 22314
(703) 549–8503

9

Domestic Violence:
Crime Prevention Begins at Home

THE OLDEST CRIMES—AND THE NEWEST

To most people, "crime" implies criminal acts or violence by strangers, the offenses that dominate the headlines and inspire calls for law and order. "Stranger crime" is, of course, one of the plagues of our time. It has produced an epidemic of fear that prevents more than half of Americans from leaving their homes alone at night. But the view that the home represents a safe refuge from crime is fraught with tragic irony. A substantial proportion of violent crimes *occur in the home:* 20 percent of assaults, 33 percent of rapes, 50 percent of murders, and close to 100 percent of child abuse, incest, and woman battering. Most of these crimes are not committed by strangers, but by friends or family members. In child abuse, the abuser is almost always one or both of the child's parents. In incest, the molester is usually the child's father or stepfather. And in wife beating, the batterer is almost always the woman's current or former husband or boyfriend. Studies show that more than 25 percent of marital partners experience violence in their relationships. In fact, a woman's risk of being beaten by her husband is an astonishing *250 percent greater* than her risk of assault on the street. (For convenience, the terms "husband" and "wife" refer to live-in relationships in general.)

171

If Eve's eating the fruit of forbidden knowledge was the original sin, then domestic violence is certainly the original crime. In the Bible, we read nothing of the random violence that makes news today, but in *The Book of Genesis* alone, Cain kills his brother and Lot commits incest with his two daughters. Until quite recently, however, prevention of domestic violence has not been a priority for society. Child abuse did not receive serious attention until the publication of "The Battered Child Syndrome" by C. Henry Kempe in 1962. Incest was unmentionable until the women's movement made sexual assault an issue in the early 1970s. And wife beating did not become an issue until the publication of *Battered Wives* by Del Martin in 1975.

Crime by strangers has inspired universal concern, but because domestic violence continues to be shrouded in myth and secrecy, it has inspired little more than confusion—if it's recognized at all. This is not only tragic, but also terribly myopic. One-third of weapons-related police calls are the result of family fights. Domestic violence is the *number one reason* people call Victim Assistance Programs. Children who are victims or witnesses of physical and/or sexual abuse learn that violence is acceptable inside the home. The clear implication is that it's also acceptable outside it. Our prisons are full of men who were beaten as children, and a study of prostitutes shows that two-thirds were victims of childhood sexual abuse. If we hope to reduce violence in society, we must make domestic-violence prevention one of our highest priorities. We must also look inside ourselves and come to grips with how *each of us* deals with anger, because violence prevention begins where violence itself begins—in the home.

THE ANGER/VIOLENCE CONTINUUM

What *is* violence? The dictionary defines it broadly: "Force exerted for the purpose of gaining or maintaining control, often involving abuse or damage." Unfortunately, in standard usage the term implies only its more extreme forms: punching, kicking, and the use of weapons. This had led to a false dichotomy between "violence" and "nonviolence." The two tend to be seen in either/or terms; but each of us has the capacity to express anger violently or nonviolently, and most acts of force occupy a broad middle ground between the two extremes, best described as points along a continuum:

NONVIOLENCE

Frank, assertive, mutually respectful negotiation

PSYCHOLOGICAL VIOLENCE

Latent irritation (sarcasm, passive aggression)
Open irritation (annoyance, raising one's voice, swearing)
Nag
Yell
Scream
Threaten physical violence

PHYSICAL VIOLENCE

Violence against objects (slam door, throw things, punch wall)
Violence against pets
Push, shove, grab person
Slap
Hit, bite, kick
Hit person with object
Beat severely, with or without object
Threaten person with weapon
Use weapon
Inflict serious weapon injury
Kill

As the level of violence increases, the proportion of people who have engaged in it decreases. Even so, violence is quite common in American homes. *Behind Closed Doors*, a comprehensive study of 2,000 families, showed that husbands and wives admitted abusing their spouses as follows:

Type of Violence	*In 1975*	*Ever*
Pushed, grabbed, shoved spouse	14%	24%
Slapped spouse	8%	18%

Type of Violence	In 1975	Ever
Threw something at spouse	7%	17%
Kicked, punched, or bit spouse	6%	9%
Hit or tried to hit spouse with object	5%	10%
Beat up spouse	2%	5%
Threatened spouse with knife or gun	1%	4%
Used knife or gun against spouse	0.5%	3%

These statistics translate into 2.3 million couples experiencing at least one severe beating, and 1.4 million, an aggravated assault. If you're surprised by this level of violence, think about the last time you got *really angry*. We all consider ourselves nonviolent, yet most of us have expressed anger physically, and many can recall coming close to losing control.

The violence people consider normal and acceptable is largely a function of their experiences while growing up. Those spanked occasionally as children generally feel all right about spanking their own children now and then. Those beaten more severely often do the same as parents.

Once domestic violence crosses the line from the psychological to the physical, it tends to increase in severity over time. Family-member homicide is a case in point. In a 1976 Police Foundation study of Kansas City, Missouri, 80 percent of family-member killings were preceded by at least one violent incident serious enough to require police intervention, and 50 percent were preceded by *five or more* police calls.

Violence is also related to social isolation. Street assailants are often loners. Similarly, those who engage in domestic violence typically have few friends and little social support.

FROM ALL WALKS OF LIFE

About 50 percent of child abuse is committed by women, usually the child's mother, but when we consider domestic violence in all its forms—child abuse, incest, and woman battering—the overwhelming majority of abusers are men. At first glance, this appears to contradict the statistics. Although 57 percent of spousal murder victims in 1980 were wives, 43 percent were husbands. But bruised, bloody, broken women, not men, are common in hospital emergency rooms, and safe houses for battered women have proliferated in recent years. So have therapy groups for violent and sexually abusive men. Battered men, like male rape victims, may be more reluctant than their female counterparts to seek help, but authorities agree that in physically or sexually abusive homes, as in all assault crimes, the vast majority of the aggressors are men. Except for female child abusers, women who commit domestic violence are almost always engaged in legitimate self-defense.

Who are the parents who batter their children? Who are the men who molest their sons and daughters, and beat their wives? The stereotype is that they are poor, uneducated, unemployed, mentally ill minority people who tend toward alcoholism, drug abuse, and street crime. A small fraction fit this description, but most appear remarkably *average and normal.*

Child-abuse psychiatrists Brandt Steele and Carl Pollack write that the parents they counsel are:

a cross-section of the population: farmers, blue- and white-collar workers, and professional people. Some are poor, some are wealthy, but most are in between. They live in metropolitan areas, small towns, and rural communities. Their educational levels range from grade school to graduate degrees. Ages range from 18 to 40, with most in their 20s. The great majority have stable (but not necessarily happy) marriages. Most are Protestant, Catholic, or Jewish. Alcohol is occasionally a source of marital conflict, but it bears no significant relationship to the episodes of child beating. Social and economic difficulties place added stress on people's lives, but such factors must be considered as incidental enhancers of child abuse, *not* as necessary and sufficient causes. We stress this because large segments of our culture still believe that child abuse occurs only among "bad people" of low socioeconomic status. This is not true.

The same could be said for families that experience incest and wife beating. Violet Chu, a counselor of battered women in San Francisco, says, "We get a surprisingly large number of calls from affluent white women: lawyers, health care professionals, businesswomen, and wives of public officials—the entire social spectrum."

SPARE THE ROD? HELP FOR ABUSIVE PARENTS

The very concept of "child abuse" assumes that children have full civil rights. For almost all of recorded history, however, children had no rights at all. Parents (i.e., fathers) had life and death authority over everyone in their households. The Bible says, "Spare the rod and spoil the child." In colonial America, fathers had the right *to kill* children they considered "incorrigible." Cultural acceptance of violence against children is also reflected in nursery rhymes:

> There was an old woman who lived in a shoe.
> She had so many children, she didn't know what to do.
> She gave them some broth without any bread,
> Then whipped them all soundly and sent them to bed.

Of course it has never been easy to raise children. Parenthood is an enormous responsibility and a source of tremendous stress, particularly for parents in their teens and early twenties. Even people who consider themselves "nonviolent" hit their children. More than 70 percent of the parents interviewed for *Behind Closed Doors* said that spanking twelve-year-olds was "normal, necessary, and good for them." Hitting a child from time to time in no way implies child abuse, but many parents go further than an occasional slap. The National Committee for the Prevention of Child Abuse estimates that 1 million children are abused every year, abuse that contributes to five thousand deaths annually—almost fourteen abuse-related child deaths *each day*.

Abusive parents may be found up and down the socioeconomic ladder, but they generally have several traits in common: About half were themselves abused as children. The younger the parents, the higher the risk. Child abuse tends to occur when parents experience severe stress from major life challenges: forced marriages, unwanted pregnancies, and job, money, and relationship problems.

Abusive parents also lack an understanding of child development. They expect the child to nurture them rather than they providing nurturance for the child:

Abusive parents, insecure and unsure of being loved, look to the child as a source of reassurance. In a reversal of normal roles, the parent acts like a frightened child, and sees the child as an adult capable of providing comfort and love. Kathy R. said, "I've never felt loved. When the baby was born, I thought he would love me. But he cried all the time, which meant he didn't love me, so I hit him." Kenny, age three weeks, was hospitalized with serious head injuries.

Abusive parents understand that their actions are wrong. One mother says, "Although I love him very much, I often do things I disapprove of. Many times after a beating, he would lie in his crib and cry himself to sleep. I'd sit there and cry and wish I could beat myself."

Child abusers may behave monstrously, but they are not monsters. By and large they raise their children as they were raised. In the 1960s, when the appalling dimensions of the problem first came to light, abusive parents were imprisoned, their children taken away from them, their families shattered forever. This approach has by no means been abandoned, but as the problem has become better understood, many states have adopted a less punitive approach, one based on intensive counseling.

With counseling, the prognosis is generally good. During the parents' therapy, the child is temporarily removed to foster care. Even if only one parent has been abusive, the couple is held jointly responsible for the problem. Treatment consists of individual and couple counseling, group therapy with other abusive parents, stress management training, and child development education. If either parent was a victim of child abuse, the therapy includes efforts to help the couple deal with the victim's parents.

Blair and Rita Justice, who lead groups for abusive parents in Texas, write: "The average length of treatment is six to nine months. The child returns home at least one month before the parents terminate therapy so newly learned child-management techniques can be applied." Another therapist writes: "Eighty percent of our parents have their children back in eight months."

With counseling, most abuse stops, and formerly abusive parents learn to let their children be children. They also learn to manage their stress more constructively. Of course situations arise that might lead to a resumption of abuse. But in communities with adequate

178 Michael Castleman

follow-up, and twenty-four-hour "parent hotlines," recidivism has been held to a minimum.

HELP FOR INCEST FAMILIES

Child sexual abuse, which usually means sexual relations between a preteen or teenaged girl and her father or stepfather, has been called "the last taboo." But until recently this so-called taboo did nothing to deter incest; all it prevented was discussion of the subject. As a result, its true prevalence is unknown. Until the 1970s, many psychologists estimated incidence at ten cases per million population. Then in 1971, Santa Clara County (San Jose), California, launched the nation's first Child Sexual Abuse Treatment Program. During its first year, the program treated thirty-five families from a population base of 1.1 million. By 1982 it was treating more than seven hundred families a year. Recent research suggests that as many as 25 percent of girls and 10 percent of boys experience some sexual molestation before adulthood.

Adults involved in incest are similar to those who physically abuse their children. A substantial proportion were themselves victims of sexual abuse. They also tend to be isolated individuals with few close friends.

Father-daughter incest imposes severe stress on the entire family. The roles of father, mother, and daughter break down, leaving everyone confused, guilty, afraid, and ashamed, especially the daughter, who is at an age when her budding sexuality requires nurturing parental guidance. But suddenly her father is forcing her to do things she can hardly imagine doing with anyone, let alone with him. The mother, if she knows at all, typically feels torn between horror at the incest and horror at the prospect of total family collapse if the police find out and send the father to jail.

Henry Giaretto, director of the Santa Clara County program, says the typical incest victim is ten years old when her father begins his sexual advances. At first his fondling feels loving, but it soon becomes confusing, and as the father progresses to intercourse, the girl recognizes his behavior as terribly wrong. The daughter typically tries to refuse, but her father won't stop. In cases that come to light, despite her shame the daughter tells her mother or another adult who calls the police.

Until recently, the criminal justice system responded to incest the same way it responds to most wrongdoing, either by doing nothing, or by overreacting. Fathers were sent to jail, daughters were removed from the family, and mothers were left to fend for themselves, their families destroyed.

Based on the Santa Clara County program, however, many communities now treat the problem differently. "When we began dealing with incest families," Giaretto recalls, "what came through loud and clear was that everyone—the daughters, mothers, and fathers—all wanted their families reunited." The fathers still serve up to a year in jail, but in most cases, the families are eventually reunited, and everyone involved participates in intensive therapy to help reconstruct their family relationships. The program accomplishes this in stages. First, the daughter, mother and father are counseled individually. Second, the mother and daughter, then the mother and father participate in joint counseling. Finally, the three are counseled together. Saving marriages is not a goal of the program, but upon release from custody, many of the fathers return to their families.

A few years after the program began, Giaretto invited several mothers who'd been through it to meet for mutual aid. Despite counseling, they still felt terribly isolated and alone with their families' traumas. The group replaced that isolation with emotional support, and as the women helped each other deal with their problems, they began to feel increased strength and resourcefulness. Eventually the fathers were invited to join. They, too, valued the group's support and felt relieved to meet other couples who shared their problems. The support-group meetings evolved into Parents United, a self-help organization for incest families. Loosely based on Alcoholics Anonymous, incest family members who have completed the counseling program lead groups (with help from professional staff) for families in treatment.

Parents United of Santa Clara County meets weekly, and fathers serving jail terms are released for the evening to attend. In eight-week cycles, participants move through several therapy groups. First is orientation, where couples confront their shock and shame. Mothers and other adults abused as children are encouraged to express their rage at the fathers, but counselors urge them to "hate the behavior, but help the man." Then there are men's and women's groups, followed by groups that emphasize husband-wife communication, parenting, and sex education. Parents United also incorporates two other organizations, Daughters and Sons United, for incest victims, and Adults Molested as Children United.

Longtime members of Parents United are quick to say that although the program is extremely helpful, the fathers and others in incest families are not necessarily transformed because of it. "With good counseling and support, the abuse stops," one mother says, "but a great deal of damage has been done that cannot be undone. You live with incest your whole life, and the potential for more abuse is always there. That's why we have 'seasoned members' groups, to help people who are past the crisis work out the everyday problems all families face."

An evaluation of Parents United families showed that 95 percent of molested children returned home within a few months. Most husbands and wives salvaged their marriages, and even those who did not generally reported better communication. Recidivism by offenders was less than 1 percent, and self-abusive behavior on the part of the molested children—truancy, running away, drug and alcohol problems, and prostitution—was held to a minimum.

"Parents United shows the tremendous power of community intervention," Giaretto says. "People in Parents United see the organization as an extended family that provides the kind of support extended families once did. But beyond Parents United, the entire community needs to help families in trouble, not ostracize them. Incest is everyone's problem whether or not it happens in your family."

TEACHING CHILDREN ABOUT SEXUAL ABUSE

Parents teach their children not to accept candy or rides from strangers, but most child molesters are men the child knows well. Child sexual abuse is clearly assaultive, but unlike adult rape, it does not necessarily involve overt force. Rather, the molester assures the child that it's okay: "Everyone does this." Or he engages in bribery: "I'll let you stay up later." Or he makes threats: "Keep this a secret or you'll get in trouble."

Sexual-abuse education begins with an explanation of the "touch continuum." Touch may feel good, confusing, or bad. A child might welcome a parent's embrace, yet feel confused by the same touch from an uncle, who seems a little too affectionate. Bad touch runs the gamut from a pinch on the cheek, through "I'll show you mine if you show me yours," to intercourse. Once the child understands the touch continuum, parents should instill three ideas:

• Even people you like can touch you in ways that feel confusing or bad.

• You have the right to refuse *any* physical contact you don't like with *anyone*.

• If anyone touches you in a way that feels confusing, tell us immediately, even if you were told to keep it a secret.

Of course this is easier said than done. Parents who wish to discuss sexual abuse with their children face many difficult questions: What does the child already know about sex? What's the right age to raise the subject? What's the best vocabulary to use? How can we warn about abuse without making the child feel uncomfortable about sexuality in general? Fortunately, these questions have been answered in *No More Secrets: Protect Your Children from Sexual Assault*, by Caren Adams and Jennifer Fay, an excellent book that equips parents to deal effectively with this difficult problem.

In addition to parents, schools also have a responsibility to teach children how to prevent unwelcome advances. Because incest usually happens in the home, the school may be the only place a child feels safe enough to mention it. A good model curriculum is available from the Child Sexual Abuse Prevention Project.

WOMAN BATTERING: THE NUMBER 1 VIOLENT CRIME

In recent years, wife beating has come to be viewed as the nation's most prevalent assault crime. In a study by the New York Victim Services Agency, battering was the most frequent crime reported. It accounted for *half* the calls from women, *40 percent more than rape, robbery, and street assault combined.*

The stereotype is that most people in battering relationships are poor, uneducated, unemployed, and largely from minority groups. The women are thought to be masochistic, their husbands, sadistic alcoholics. But like child abuse and incest, battering occurs in all walks of life. The socioeconomic scope of the problem becomes clear when one examines the recent proliferation of services for battered women—and for men who batter—in affluent communities, for example, the suburbs of Washington, D.C., and in Marin, one of the wealthiest counties in California.

Like child abusers, men who batter are usually neither sadistic nor mentally ill. Wife beating is often associated with alcohol, but only a fraction of batterers are alcoholics. The vast majority are employed, some in professional positions. Outwardly, most batterers are "regular guys." In fact, battered women often cite the batterer's "charm and sensitivity" as two of his endearing qualities. But these men have split personalities. As the stress in their lives builds, Dr. Jekyll explodes into Mr. Hyde.

Like all those involved in domestic violence, men and women in battering relationships tend to share certain psychological traits. Psychotherapist Lenore Walker, author of *The Battered Woman*, lists the following as common:

- Both partners have low self-esteem. Even if they have good jobs, they feel frustrated and stuck.

- Both believe in traditional sex roles. The relationship is male-dominated.

- The batterer denies responsibility for his violence. He blames it on provocation by the woman, who accepts responsibility for her husband's actions.

- The man is extremely jealous and possessive, the woman passive and resigned to the situation.

- The man uses sex aggressively to enhance his self-esteem. The woman uses it to establish intimacy.

- Both experience severe stress. The man uses alcohol and violence to cope. The woman uses psychosomatic complaints and medication.

WHY DO THEY STAY?

Abused infants and young incest victims cannot leave their families, but battered women are adults. Why don't they walk out? Many do. Physical abuse is cited by wives as a factor in *half* of all divorces.

Yet many battered women remain in relationships with men who brutalize them, often for years, which leads to accusations that they're "stupid, crazy, and masochistic." Incredulous reactions are understandable—until one begins to appreciate the dynamics of battering relationships.

One reason many women stay is that they lack the money and job skills to leave. Even when they work outside the home, the man often controls the money and makes the financial decisions. The checking account is often in his name only, and he makes the woman account for every penny she spends. Many battered women go to great lengths to squirrel away small change without their husbands' knowledge, then eventually use their nest eggs to escape.

Then there are the costs of leaving versus the benefits of staying. Like the rest of us, battered women face trade-offs. Consider work: Some jobs involve high levels of stress, verbal abuse, physical pain— even risk of death—yet people put up with them because the pay is decent, the fringe benefits attractive, and the routine familiar, even if some bruises are part of the bargain.

But what about a marriage where bruises become broken bones? Part of the reason battered women endure repeated beatings has to do with their previous experience with domestic violence. Few families are completely violence-free. Of course tolerance of some family violence in no way implies acceptance of wife beating, but in the large majority of homes where hitting is not absolutely proscribed, the distinction between "normal" and "excessive" violence is merely a matter of degree.

Another reason involves the split personalities battered women typically attribute to their husbands. Many rationalize their husbands' outbursts by focusing on their positive traits: "He's really a good man; but now and then he loses his temper."

Because battered women accept the traditional women's role of taking responsibility for the actions of everyone in the family, they typically blame themselves, not the man, for the violence in their lives. They think in terms of "if only." "If only I were a better homemaker, he wouldn't hit me." They also tend to agree with husbands who blame them for real or imagined infractions. Violet Chu, a counselor with the San Francisco agency, W.O.M.A.N., Inc., says this story is typical: "She sees him getting angry and gets terrified that he's about to blow up. It makes her nervous, so she spills some-

thing, which sets him off. 'You're so clumsy! You're such a slob!'
Then he hits her and blames her for it. 'Now see what you made me
do!?' Rather than getting angry, the woman says, 'You're right; I'll
try to be more careful.' "

Acceptance of battering also involves social isolation. "Battered
women," Chu explains, "typically feel imprisoned in their homes
with nowhere to turn, without friends or support. If they overcome
the shame they feel about being beaten, and raise the subject, quite
often no one believes them, not even their own families. The
woman's family knows the husband as a decent person. They may
blame *her* for any violence, saying she must have provoked her husband's temper. They often tell her to 'work harder' on the marriage.
Then she feels even more isolated." Religious objections to divorce
also play a role in making some women feel that there's no way out.

Many battered women stay because despite their husbands' "tempers" they feel deeply committed to the relationship. They often pity
the man and hope they can help him change. "In general," Chu
says, "battered women sincerely believe that their role is to 'stand by
their man.' The times he's charming keeps them hoping he'll stop
hitting."

Finally, leaving may not help. Many batterers pursue their wives
and continue to beat them. Fully *half* the women who contact
W.O.M.A.N., Inc., do not live with their abuser. That's why shelters
for battered women don't publish their addresses.

THE THREE STAGES OF DOMESTIC ASSAULT

Like the three-stage pattern of street assault, battering also involves three phases. First is the build-up of stress and tension, then
comes the explosion, and finally, remorse. During Phase One, the
batterer becomes spiteful, verbally abusive, and faultfinding. He
blames the woman for every little thing and threatens violence. The
woman recognizes that she's "in for it." In Phase Two, the assault
may last a few moments or go on for hours. It may include sexual assault and the use of weapons. Then comes Phase Three—sincere remorse on the part of the batterer. His fury spent, he begs his wife's
forgiveness and promises never to hit her again if she'll just stay with

him and help him change. Contrite batterers often shower their wives with tenderness, gifts, and promises to go into therapy. But then the stress buildup begins anew. The tenderness becomes verbal abuse. The gifts may be destroyed during the next outburst, and very few batterers get therapy while their wives remain with them.

"When trying to break the cycle," Chu explains, "Phase Three is the problem. The man is sincere in his remorse and the woman really wants to believe him. She keeps hoping and he keeps hitting. Over time, the violence escalates. The more he knows he's 'got her,' the more frequent and severe the beatings become. After a few years, Phase Three disappears. There's no remorse anymore, no promises to change, just an endless cycle of stress and explosions. It's at that point that the woman finally realizes she can't change him. It's also at that point that husbands and wives sometimes kill each other."

A CHECKLIST OF WARNING SIGNS

The Jekyll-and-Hyde nature of the typical batterer's personality means that it's often difficult to discern the early-warning signs of potentially abusive relationships. The following checklist, drawn from *The Battered Woman* and W.O.M.A.N., Inc., should help women identify problem relationships.

- Does he negotiate differences of opinion in good faith, or does he try to browbeat you into submission?

- Does he bottle up stress and anger, and lose his temper frequently and inappropriately?

- Is he excessively jealous and possessive? Does he expect you to spend all your free time with him? Does he try to limit your time with others?

- Does he use alcohol to cope with stress? Does it make him violent?
- Has he ever threatened you with violence? Hit you?

- Does he appear to have a split personality? Do you get a sense of "overkill" from his kindness or his cruelty?
- Do you feel a sense of dread when he gets angry?

- Does he hold a rigid belief in traditional sex-role stereotypes?
- Does the three-phase cycle of domestic violence describe your relationship?

A man might display a few of these traits and *not* become a batterer, and depending on the circumstances, occasional physical outbursts by themselves do not necessarily make anyone a wife beater. But if you have ever been subjected to physical abuse, consider calling one of the organizations listed in Resources.

BATTERING IS DIFFERENT FROM FIGHTING

Arguments between lovers are a normal, healthy part of every intimate relationship. In fact, marriage counselors generally become concerned about relationships that do not experience periodic "blow-ups." Conflict per se is not the issue. It's *how* the two people deal with their differences, and with stress in the relationship in general. Fortunately, it's quite possible to fight furiously, yet lovingly and nonviolently. The skills involved are relatively easy to learn. Two guides are especially useful: *The Intimate Enemy* by George Bach and Peter Wyden is the classic in the field. Bach and Wyden celebrate conflict as a potentially creative force, and equip couples with sensible rules and useful tools for fair fighting. *A Couple's Guide to Communication* by John Gottman, Cliff Notarius, Jonni Gonso, and Howard Markman is also excellent. The authors studied the ways in which couples in mutually satisfying relationships resolved their differences—all had weathered many serious conflicts—and devised exercises based on their successful techniques. If you feel at all frustrated by communication problems in your relationship, these two books are a good place to start. If they do not help sufficiently, consider counseling.

OPTIONS FOR BATTERED WOMEN

First, call one of the many hotlines that provide assistance. If you don't know whom to call in your community, request a referral from a local rape crisis center, church group, chapter of the National Organization for Women (NOW), or your local district attorney's office. The Center for Women's Policy Studies and W.O.M.A.N., Inc., both provide referrals to shelters all over the country.

Another good resource is the book *Getting Free: A Handbook for Women in Abusive Relationships* by Ginny NiCarthy, which helps battered women sort out their options.

If he hits you, consider having him arrested for assault. Counselors often urge this, but it may not be as easy as it sounds. Traditionally, police have shown little enthusiasm for arresting men accused of domestic assault. They receive little training in domestic crime compared with stranger crime. If young officers learn anything about domestic violence, it's that if they intervene, *their* risk of injury is high. Intervention in domestic disputes accounts for about 25 percent of all police injuries. Surveys also show that police generally consider it futile to arrest batterers. They believe the men quickly return home and beat the women more severely in retaliation. Police complain that most women drop charges against their husbands, making any arrest "a waste." Police also say that temporary restraining orders that forbid the batterer to approach the woman are impossible to enforce.

Fortunately, the police response to battering is changing. In 1978, the New York City Police Department changed its orders for dealing with domestic disturbances from "arrest on officer discretion" to "arrest on spousal request." According to New York Police Academy Instructor William Feeley, if the woman wants her husband arrested, New York police must make the arrest. As a result, arrests of suspected batterers have increased significantly.

In 1982, New York's Victim Services Agency released the results of a three-year study of the effects of the program on battered women. Contrary to traditional police assumptions, the report showed that even when the women dropped assault charges, insistence on the arrest reduced their risk of future beatings. Fifty-three of the 112 victims (47 percent) said the threat of further legal action deterred their husbands from beating them. The report also said that upon release, usually after twenty-four hours in jail, most husbands did not administer retaliatory beatings.

"Even when a woman doesn't prosecute," Violet Chu says, "arrest is crucial. It's an important step toward overcoming the feelings of powerlessness that keep her trapped in the battering relationship. It also gives her time—even if only a little—to collect her thoughts, call an agency, get counseling, and maybe go to a safe house."

Arrest of suspected batterers might also help reduce the spousal murder rate. The authors of the study that showed that 80 percent of spousal homicides in Kansas City were preceded by at least one previous police call, suggested that early intervention, i.e., arrest, could help break the cycle of violence and prevent its escalation to murder. A growing number of police departments now arrest batterers on spousal request.

Although he had no figures on changes in police injuries since the new policy has gone into effect, Police Academy Instructor Feeley said he felt that injuries were "less likely" when officers were quick to arrest suspected batterers: "In domestic disputes, officers sustain their injuries when attempting to mediate the problem. But mediation puts them in the middle of a volatile situation. Under the new orders, officers go in with clearer objectives—if the woman requests arrest, they make the arrest. That's a much less ambiguous position, one less likely to result in injury."

Traditional police skepticism about temporary restraining orders also appears to be unfounded. Lenore Walker's study of 125 battered women showed that 80 percent of those who obtained restraining orders said their husbands obeyed them.

OPTIONS FOR MEN WHO BATTER

Men who hit their wives must stop it. They must learn to express anger and work out disagreements nonviolently. In recent years, many counseling services have been established to help men overcome domestic violence. Emerge, in Boston, is a good source of national referrals.

Another approach is to use the workbook *Learning to Live Without Violence* by Daniel Sonkin and Michael Durphy. It outlines a fourteen-week program that helps men recognize and control their anger, deal with the stress in their lives, and communicate more effectively in their relationships.

Sonkin, a longtime leader of groups for batterers, says, "It's not easy for men to overcome violence, but if a man takes responsibility for his violence and stays in a group six to twelve months, he can learn to handle his anger differently. Our follow-up shows that some men have eliminated violence from their relationships, and that others have reduced it considerably. Of course, we live in a violent culture, and our group occupies only a tiny fraction of the man's life, but I'm optimistic. I've seen men change."

"MAYBE IT'S NONE OF MY BUSINESS, BUT . . ."

Domestic crime prevention, like *all* crime prevention, is everybody's business. If you can see ten other homes from your own front door, chances are that some form of domestic violence has taken place in at least one of them. Domestic crime affects not only those directly involved in child abuse, incest, and battering, but all of us. It's impossible to feel safe if you hear screaming down the street. And even when the screams are inaudible, if there are children, especially boys, in an abusive household, they may express their anger and confusion outside their homes.

Comprehensive crime prevention *must* include a strong focus on domestic violence; without it, neighborhood programs can only go so far. Violence in any home should be seen as unacceptable to *everyone* in the neighborhood. Unfortunately, some people say, "It's none of my business." One witness to the Kitty Genovese murder said she didn't call the police because she "thought it was a domestic quarrel." The traditional belief that "a man's home is his castle" is still firmly entrenched. Neighbors are often reluctant to intervene, even when they know that the castle down the street has become a dungeon for those who live there.

Despite the tendency not to intervene, a great many people do. They refer someone in the family to a social service agency or to the police. A substantial proportion of cases of child abuse, incest, and wife beating have *always* come to light because of concerned neighbors and friends.

One common denominator in all forms of domestic abuse is social isolation. Neighborhood crime-prevention programs can be crucial in reducing that isolation and giving victims—and offenders—the support they need to overcome their problems. Local groups can do a great deal, but effective intervention in domestic violence requires more than just community action. The criminal justice system and social service agencies must make it one of their highest priorities. Unfortunately, public officials across the political spectrum have not placed domestic violence high enough on the public agenda to finance the necessary effort. This failure is tragic, but it's only one reason why neither the liberal nor conservative crime-control programs have produced significant results.

Resources:

The National Committee to Prevent Child Abuse
332 South Michigan Ave., Suite 1250
Chicago, IL 60604
(312) 663–3520

Publishes resources and conducts media campaigns to educate the public about child abuse.

Parents United
P.O. Box 952
San Jose, CA 95108
(408) 280–5055

Ninety chapters around the U.S. and Canada. Provides assistance to new chapters and publishes a newsletter ($12 for nine issues).

No More Secrets: Protecting Your Child from Sexual Assault
by Caren Adams and Jennifer Fay
1981, 90 pages, $3.95
Impact Publishers
P.O. Box 1094
San Luis Obispo, CA 93406

The book for parents.

Child Sexual Abuse Prevention Project Curriculum
by Cordelia Kent
1979, 120 pages, $8.00
Hennepin County Attorney's Office
2000 Government Center
Minneapolis, MN 55487
(612) 348–8835
Contains sections for elementary, junior high, and high school, with activities for each age group.

The Battered Woman
by Lenore E. Walker, Ph.D.
1980, 270 pages, $4.95
Harper Colophon Books
10 East 53rd St.
New York, NY 10022
A revealing psychological perspective on the problem.

The Intimate Enemy: How to Fight Fair in Love and Marriage
by George R. Bach, Ph.D., and Peter Wyden
1968, 384 pages, $2.45
Avon Books
959 Eighth Ave.
New York, NY 10019
The classic book on fair fighting in relationships.

A Couple's Guide to Communication
by John Gottman, Cliff Notarius, Jonni Gonso, & Howard Markman
1976, 220 pages, $6.95
Research Press
2612 North Mattis Ave.
Champaign, IL 61820
Helps improve the quality of all communication.

The Center for Women's Policy Studies
2000 P St., N.W.
Washington, DC 20036
(202) 872–1770
Open Monday through Friday, 9 A.M. to 5 P.M. Referrals to counseling and safe houses around the United States.

Women Organized to Make Abuse Nonexistent (W.O.M.A.N.),
    Inc.
2940 - 16th St.
San Francisco, CA 94103
24-HOUR HOTLINE: (415) 864–4722

Referrals to counseling and safe houses around the U.S.

Getting Free: A Handbook for Women in Abusive Relationships
by Ginny NiCarthy
1982, 272 pages, $7.95
Seal Press
312 South Washington St.
Seattle, WA 98104

A valuable resource for any woman in a problem relationship.

Emerge, Men Counseling Men on Domestic Violence
25 Huntington Ave., Room 206
Boston, MA 02116
(617) 267–7690

Referrals to counseling services for batterers. The manual "Organizing Services for Men Who Batter," is available for $25.

Learning to Live Without Violence
by Daniel J. Sonkin, Ph.D., and Michael Durphy, M.D.
1982, 124 pages, $10.00
Volcano Press
330 Ellis St.
San Francisco, CA 94102

10

Liberals *vs.* Conservatives:
The Conventional Wisdom Reconsidered

THE MISSING LINK: SECONDARY PREVENTION

What *really* prevents crime? The most dramatic and cost-effective approaches include street awareness to prevent violent crimes; target-hardening to prevent property crimes; and neighborhood organizing to build community cohesion and assist in dealing with domestic violence. Going back to the analogy of epidemic disease, successful crime prevention depends on strengthening "host resistance" to the "germs" of crime, that is, on *secondary prevention*. If, as a nation, we placed more emphasis on this kind of prevention, the crime rate could be reduced quickly and substantially. There would be fewer criminals to pursue and imprison and fewer victims to care for. Our social problems would still be with us, but with the crime rate way down, they would look less overwhelming, and scarce resources could be used more wisely to deal with them.

RETHINKING THE LIBERAL AGENDA

Liberals argue that the best way to deal with crime is through primary prevention—eliminating poverty, unemployment, and racial discrimination. These problems are quite serious; they deserve higher priority for government money than they have received in recent years. But to what extent do they really *cause* crime? The evidence suggests that they contribute less to the crime problem than most liberals believe.

The immediate cause of stranger crime is the combination of impulse and opportunity. Poverty, unemployment, and discrimination can certainly contribute to impulsiveness, but their effect on criminal *opportunity* is not at all clear; hence the difficulty in demonstrating a persuasive cause-and-effect relationship.

This is not to say that we should abandon the struggle for social justice. Quite the contrary; we should redouble our efforts, not because full employment and social equality would necessarily eradicate crime—they wouldn't—but rather because they are *right*.

"THE BALLAD OF PRETTY BOY FLOYD"

If poverty and unemployment were major causes of crime, neither the 7-Eleven nor Detroit programs would have worked. Yet both produced substantial reductions in crime. Conversely, during the mid-1970s, the Sunbelt had little poverty and unemployment. If these factors were important causes of crime, the boomtowns of the South and Southwest should have had the nation's lowest crime rates. But as they prospered, their crime rates soared.

Poverty and unemployment are key factors of a community's material circumstances, but its crime rate is most closely associated with something else, neighborhood cohesion. Both economic bust and boom may destroy an area's sense of community. When that happens, the crime rate rises. But when community cohesion increases the crime rate drops, whether or not the area is rich or poor, working or unemployed.

The standard liberal belief that poverty causes crime has an important—and erroneous—corollary, that poor people commit the nation's most serious crimes. Poor, unemployed, minority criminals are clearly those most likely to wind up in prison, but that reveals less about crime than about the inequities of the legal system. Losses from the most lucrative white-collar crimes—investment fraud, embezzlement, and counterfeiting—run as high as $40 billion each year. The poor and unemployed could not commit these crimes even if they wanted to. The only people in positions to do so are those whose occupations provide the opportunity. "The Ballad of Pretty Boy Floyd," a Depression-era folk song about a bank-robbing Robin Hood, puts it this way: "Some'll rob you with a six-gun/ And some with a fountain pen." Consider the nation's most costly theft crime, income tax evasion. For 1981, the IRS estimated that 25 percent of taxpayers defrauded the government out of a staggering $87 billion, *four times* the cost of all theft crimes combined. With 95 million returns filed, tax evasion occurred on about 24 million of them, for an average theft of $3,625 per fraudulent return—30 percent more than the take from the average bank robbery.

None of this is meant to dismiss the gravity of robbery, rape, and burglary. But it's clear that if the criminal justice system treated white-collar criminals the way it treats burglars, our prisons would not be filled with poor people as they are now. They would contain a cross section of the population.

The stress of unemployment can certainly contribute to the impulse to commit both stranger crime and domestic violence, and most liberals promote jobs programs—in part because they believe that full employment is morally desirable, and in part because they believe it prevents crime. Full employment *is* morally just, but its effects on the crime rate are by no means clear. The Crary/St. Mary's neighborhood cut its crime rate in half at a time when Detroit had one of the nation's highest unemployment rates. And the most prevalent violent crimes—child abuse, incest, and woman battering—occur across the socioeconomic spectrum. In addition, many jobs *increase* opportunities for crime. This is certainly true in the case of white-collar crime. It's also true for youth crime.

University of Iowa researchers examined the juvenile delinquency records for 1974–1980 of Racine, Wisconsin, a multiracial city they called "a socioeconomic microcosm of the United States." One finding: "Contrary to the notion that employment deters delinquency, young men who were employed had *more* police contacts and higher seriousness [of crimes committed]" than their unemployed counterparts. Why? Because working was associated with increased access to an automobile, which increased the youths' criminal opportunities.

This is not to dismiss the value of youth employment, but rather to argue for jobs that not only provide income, but also reinforce positive social values. This is an important element of Detroit's Junior Police Cadet program, which provides high-school credit and summer jobs to young people who work as escorts for elderly residents of public housing projects. Cadet Supervisor Sergeant Jerry Neal says, "Most youth employment programs put kids to work cutting weeds and picking up litter. But how does that work make a kid feel? What does it teach? These kids don't just need jobs, they need to feel they're making a contribution."

CUT CRIME TO REDUCE RACIAL PREJUDICE

Although whites commit 70 percent of index offenses (and a much higher proportion of white-collar crimes), black people commit more than twice as many index crimes as their numbers in the population would predict. Both individual bigotry and institutional racism can fuel the impulse to commit crime—one reason why recruitment of minority officers is so important. In cities that have experienced racial strife, integration of the police force has contributed to significant decreases in racial tensions.

But the liberal program is disturbingly fatalistic about crime and prejudice. Many liberals seem to rationalize black criminality by saying that after four hundred years of black slavery and a hundred and twenty of freedom, which at times has offered only scant improvement over servitude, it will take many more generations for the wounds of racism to heal. While this is true, a more constructive approach would be to introduce neighborhood crime prevention into *every* community. This would mean that people of every race and ethnic group would take responsibility for their own personal and neighborhood safety. Since black people have the highest victimization rate, they also have the most to gain from self-help efforts. And the substantial decrease in crime likely to result from a serious national crime-prevention initiative would probably do more to change prejudicial attitudes than all the political rhetoric that passes for action on racial issues today.

"DON'T BLAME ME, BLAME SOCIETY"

Blaming crime on society is an extension of the fatalism just mentioned. No individual can do much about poverty, unemployment, and racism. But the consistent success of crime-prevention programs proves there's a *great deal* each of us can do to become safer.

Like crime prevention, successful criminal rehabilitation also depends on instilling a sense of personal responsibility for one's actions. One example is the Delancey Street Foundation of San Francisco, a self-help residential program for former criminals, prostitutes, and drug addicts. The average Delancey Street resident has spent eleven years in prison. Many could be termed victims of social inequality, but in the organization's group-therapy sessions, anyone who blamed society for his or her wrongdoing would face intense criticism. John Maher, Delancey Street's tough-talking, ex-heroin-addict founder and president, favors social change, but insists that residents change themselves first:

Society is all screwed up. We're going to change that, but before we do, we gotta understand that we ex-cons and addicts ain't nice either— that's a myth! Trouble is, some of you "nice" people believe that ex-cons and dope fiends are "misunderstood." You look at them and say, "I know you've had a hard life." *What life?* Selling dope to kids and hanging out with Scumbags Anonymous? They tell you, "No one ever treated me like a human being." Question is, where did they get the idea that someone who mugs old women *is* a human being? We're pretty twisted. We gotta untwist ourselves by taking personal responsibility for our own change.

Delancey Street residents "untwist" themselves through group therapy, going to school, and by working for one of the organization's small, self-sustaining businesses: a restaurant, a moving company, and a construction company, among others. Although this approach is deeply rooted in Yankee self-reliance, many have called Delancey Street "radical." Maher replies: "What's really radical about us is that we *work* for a living."

Delancey Street's fiercely independent self-help posture highlights another problem with the liberal approach to crime, its creation of unhealthy dependencies on government programs. People in need certainly deserve public support, but throwing money at social problems undermines the initiative and self-respect of those on the receiving end. To guard against this, Delancey Street's adult program has refused all public support. "We take no government money," Copresident Mimi Silbert says, "because we believe in teaching self-reliance. Pride and dignity come from earning your own way." At Delancey Street's businesses, participants work long hours for unenviable wages. They could probably do better financially on welfare, food stamps, and hustling. But Delancey Street provides income more precious than dollars. It instills self-respect, something usually quite new to the residents. Most have spent their lives labeled as "losers" fit only for prison or government handouts.

The government cannot "deliver" the nation from its social problems anymore than the police can deliver us from crime. Funding that creates dependencies on the whims of legislators rarely empowers people to gain greater control over their lives. It often socializes them into further helplessness. This is not to argue against social programs, but in favor of efforts that contribute to self-reliance and resourcefulness—for example, neighborhood crime prevention. People who help reduce their communities' crime rates experience a personal satisfaction money can't buy. Success against crime confers authority and builds self-confidence, which fosters political assertiveness. It's no coincidence that the Delancey Street Foundation has become politically influential in San Francisco.

RETHINKING THE CONSERVATIVE AGENDA

Conservatives argue that the best way to deal with crime is through tertiary prevention: more police with more sophisticated equipment, and more prisons and longer sentences.

The threat of punishment clearly helps control some impulses to commit certain crimes. Most of the 75 percent of taxpayers who file legitimate income tax returns, for example, say the threat of an audit helps keep them honest. The threat of punishment may discourage some of the impulses, but because it has little effect on criminal *op-*

portunities, conservatives have been unable to show any persuasive cause-and-effect relationship between the crime rate and increases in police strength and prison terms.

THE POLICE DON'T PREVENT CRIME,
THE PEOPLE DO

The 7-Eleven chain cut its crime rate in half without any help from police. In Detroit, the police insisted that for Neighborhood Watch to work, their role had to be secondary to the community's. Police are to crime what doctors are to illness. Both work primarily after the fact. Police can be valuable crime-prevention consultants, just as physicians can provide important health advice. But each of us must take primary responsibility for our health and our personal safety. In recent years, more and more police have adopted this view—not just crime-prevention officers, but some of the nation's top police officers, notably Patrick V. Murphy.

Murphy might be described as the police officer's police officer. His father and two brothers were New York City cops. During his forty-year career, Murphy rose from beat patrolman in Brooklyn to police commissioner of Syracuse, Detroit, New York, and Washington, D.C. He was the first director of the Law Enforcement Assistance Administration, and since 1973 has been president of the Police Foundation in Washington, D.C., the nation's foremost police research organization. Murphy has experienced police work from bottom to top, and in his autobiography he writes: "The relationship between police work and crime control is often coincidental. I do not think that more cops [or] a repressive law-and-order approach are the answer."

Murphy has long been particularly critical of car-based preventive patrol, the major activity of most police. This opinion put him at odds with conventional police wisdom, but in agreement with the report of the 1967 Presidential Crime Commission, which found that enormous variations in cities' deployment of police on preventive patrol had no effect on their crime rates. This conclusion raised howls of protest from most police chiefs, who support vehicular patrol as the key to rapid response and, therefore, to crime control. The controversy led the Police Foundation to launch the first scientific test of preventive patrol's effectiveness.

The year-long (1972–73) experiment took place in Kansas City, Missouri, in a thirty-two-square-mile, high-crime area with a racially mixed, low-to-moderate-income population of 148,000. In five of the area's fifteen patrol sectors, the number of cars on preventive patrol was doubled and sometimes tripled. In five sectors, preventive patrol was completely eliminated; patrol cars went there only in response to calls for assistance. And in the remaining five sectors, preventive patrol continued as it had for years. The public was not informed of these changes. Researchers monitored police crime statistics, and also conducted victimization surveys.

The results demolished police patrol. The superpatrolled sectors experienced no decrease in crime, and residents expressed no decrease in fear. The extra patrols did not displace crime to the less patrolled sectors, nor did the crime rate increase in the sectors where preventive patrol was completely eliminated. The researchers concluded that routine preventive patrol had no effect on the crime rate, police response times, or citizen fear.

Murphy commented: "The power of the study was enhanced by the typicality of Kansas City. Its problems are national problems. It ranks close to [other cities] in aggravated assault and murder rates. If routine patrolling does not work in Kansas City, there is little reason to believe it can work anywhere in the United States."

The Kansas City results were corroborated the following year in Nashville, Tennessee, where a special antiburglary unit saturated one of three patrol areas. The two control areas remained under routine patrol. After three months, the burglary rate did not decline in the superpatrolled area, nor did it increase in the control areas.

The only thing preventive patrol really prevents is citizen interaction with police. Murphy believes that police should drastically reduce their reliance on preventive patrol and return to the days when officers spent most of their time getting to know local people by walking beats:

Patrol cars are indispensable, but overrelied on. The rapid-response emphasis has neglected the need for citizen participation in crime control. The vast majority of residents of *any* community—black, white, or brown—are not only law-abiding, but also potentially law-assisting. The job of any officer is to enlist [community support] in the struggle against crime [and] . . . to make friends.

The problem with befriending residents is that it's almost impossible to do from inside a patrol car. "As a young officer," Murphy writes, "it took me quite some time to latch onto a radio car. But it didn't take long to realize that [it] was a losing proposition. Policing a neighborhood from a car is like trying to relate to an alien society from behind the windows of a low-hovering flying saucer."

Murphy also inveighs against what he calls "the detective mystique." Movies, television, and popular fiction have persuaded us that detectives always get their man. The fact is, detectives rarely solve crimes. Murphy writes: "For all their uncanny ability to make headlines and friends in the press corps, detectives make an arguably insignificant contribution to crime control." As New York Police Commissioner, Murphy asked the Crime Analysis Section to calculate the Detective Bureau's arrest rate. The results, he writes, were "devastating: 5.6 percent for robberies, 1.9 percent for burglaries, and 2.2 percent for grand larceny." A Rand Corporation analysis of detective work agrees: "It is a rare event when a crime is solved through the clever piecing together of a fragile chain of evidence."

The Detroit and West Philadelphia examples show that police usually catch criminals when local residents tell them whom to arrest. One reason the nation's police arrest rate hovers disappointingly around 20 percent is that so many people feel uncomfortable reporting suspicious activity to officers they perceive as strangers. This reluctance is not surprising given the law enforcement commitment to policing from behind patrol car windows. Why say anything to nameless men and women whose standard operating procedures are almost as hit-and-run as the criminals'? On the other hand, foot patrol increases contact between police and the public. It encourages officers to provide what people really want: crime-prevention advice, counseling, and referrals to social services. Despite the TV image of police work, officers spend only a small fraction of their time actually pursuing criminals. Most crimes are neighborhood events. If they are solved, neighborhood people usually deserve the credit.

PUNISHMENT: SOME WORKS BUT
PRISON DOESN'T

The real experts on imprisonment are those who have done time. Ex-convicts almost universally agree that prison is no crime deterrent. Ray Johnson of 7-Eleven writes: "Prisons neither punish nor rehabilitate. At worst, they're training programs for crime skills. At best, all they do is teach people how to get along in prison. The problem, of course, is that the only place you can use that training is behind bars."

The research agrees. A report by the National Council on Crime and Delinquency concludes: "There appears to be no significant relationship between crime rates and incarceration rates." A study by the National Academy of Sciences showed that New York, California, and Massachusetts would have to *double* their prison populations to even hope to achieve a modest 10 percent reduction in crime. "Prison," Santa Clara County, California, Superior Court Judge Peter Stone says, "is the easy way out. It's the quick fix that solves nothing."

Psychological research has shown that punishment *can* change behavior, but only if it's immediate, certain, and severe. In recent years, punishment has become more certain and severe, but given a commitment to "innocent until proven guilty," punishment can *never be immediate*. As a result, it cannot be relied upon to prevent much crime.

In general, conservatives argue for less government spending, but their crime-control program costs a fortune. Ray Johnson writes: "It cost several hundred thousand dollars for [California] to 'rehabilitate' me. The truth is I got rehabilitated despite [twenty-five years in prison]. I don't think a nickel's worth of prison did me any good. Hell, you could send every prisoner in the country to Harvard for what it costs to keep them locked up."

Imprisonment now costs taxpayers $20,000 per prisoner per year, more than the cost of a year at the finest universities. In addition, the cost of imprisonment has risen 40 percent faster than inflation. What has this enormous investment returned? The near-universal answer from reformed criminals and criminal justice authorities alike is "not much."

Some people will always have to be incarcerated, but as the Baby Boom generation grows older, imprisonment should decline. At present, our prisons are overcrowded, but new prison construction is not the most cost-effective answer. It would make more sense to invest some of the funds earmarked for new prisons in grassroots crime-prevention efforts to keep as many people as possible out of the penal system by preventing crimes *before they occur.*

TV VIOLENCE: CAUSE OF FEAR BUT NOT CRIME

Across the political spectrum, many people believe that television violence is an important cause of crime. There is certainly no lack of violence on TV. Even the most devoted apologist for the networks would have to call much of it tasteless and gratuitous. And when real people commit real crimes that are exact duplicates of fictional crimes broadcast a day or two earlier, it would be difficult to argue that the two events are entirely coincidental. Television violence, like poverty and unemployment, may stimulate impulsive actions and contribute to some real-life violence now and then, but the evidence shows that it is not an important cause of crime. At the same time, however, television's portrayals of crime and police work significantly distort our thinking and, as a result, interfere with crime-prevention efforts.

There can be no question that television influences behavior. Its very *purpose* is to persuade viewers to purchase the advertised products. Many studies show that children exposed to large amounts of TV violence are more likely than their unexposed counterparts to engage in aggressive play. But aggressive play is quite different from crime. Other studies show that children understand that TV programs are fantasies, not to be taken seriously. And when victims of crimes that copied TV crimes have sued the programs' producers, the courts have consistently held that the producers are not liable.

In 1982, the National Coalition on Television Violence (NCTV), a monitoring group in Decatur, Illinois, announced that TV violence had increased 25 percent from 1980 to 1981 to an all-time high. Yet, since the mid-1970s, arrests of juveniles, those considered most likely to be influenced by TV violence, *declined* almost 19 percent. The steady increase in TV violence in the face of declining juvenile arrests and the success of community-based crime prevention strongly suggests that crime and TV violence are not as closely linked as groups like NCTV claim.

Although no direct relationship has ever been demonstrated between television violence and crime, there *is* a serious problem with TV mayhem. Television distorts our thinking by reinforcing the notion that violence is a normal, acceptable way to resolve conflicts. The problem is not TV violence per se but the way it's presented. The mini-series "Roots" showed the violence of slavery more explicitly than television ever had; "Holocaust" did the same for the violence of Nazi Germany. But that violence was presented as reprehensible. Far from causing crime, TV violence might have an ultimately prosocial impact if presented as tragic and unacceptable.

Television also distorts our thinking about the crime rate. Studies by George Gerbner of the University of Pennsylvania show that television promotes a "mean-world syndrome." The crime rate on TV is *ten times* the nation's actual crime rate, and during prime time it's even higher: "Fifty-five percent of prime-time characters are involved in violence each week; in reality, the figure should be less than one percent. In all demographic groups, heavy TV viewers overestimate their [risk] of criminal violence."

What is television's answer to crime? More police. Programs about supercops dominate prime time. But as we have seen, in the fight against crime, the police play a supporting role at best. TV cops fire their weapons frequently, but according to Patrick Murphy, most officers do not fire at criminal suspects *even once* in a twenty-year career. Television—and the news media in general—heighten anxieties about victimization, while at the same time misleading people about the best ways to deal with crime.

OPPORTUNITY CONTROL: MORE COST-EFFECTIVE THAN IMPULSE CONTROL

The conventional approaches to crime attempt to control the impulse to do wrong. Liberals focus on eliminating social injustice.

Conservatives seek to instill fear of capture and punishment. Impulse control is certainly a vital component of crime prevention, but opportunity control is more important.

We need to strike a better balance in the struggle to control crime. Neither the liberal nor the conservative approach has done much to reduce the crime rate; meanwhile, both programs are quite costly. We need to unite around the crime-prevention approaches with clearest proven cost-effectiveness. Political debate about the crime problem is healthy, but it becomes counterproductive when our differences obscure the simple, economical, common-sense approaches everyone can support, the solutions that work best.

Resource:

Commissioner: A View from the Top of American Law Enforcement by Patrick V. Murphy and Thomas Plate.
1977, 280 pages, $10.95
Simon and Schuster
1230 Avenue of the Americas
New York, NY 10020
The best book on police work.

11

Guns vs. Gun Control: Neither as Effective as Secondary Prevention

None of the most effective crime-prevention strategies—street awareness, target-hardening, community organizing, and domestic-violence prevention—have anything to do with either armed deterrence or gun control. The 7-Eleven chain and Detroit's Crary/St. Mary's neighborhood cut their crime rates in half without arming anyone and without restricting the general availability of firearms, specifically handguns.

Their experiences stand in sharp contrast to *both* conventional perspectives on weapons and crime—the progun view that guns, specifically handguns, deter crime, and the antigun view that they contribute to it. However, they agree with the findings of the most comprehensive study of the gun issue currently available, the 1981 Justice Department report, "Weapons, Crime, and Violence in America" (published in book form as *Under the Gun*), by James D. Wright and Peter Rossi of the University of Massachusetts at Amherst. Their three-year investigation reviewed the entire social science literature on guns and crime. Wright and Rossi, who began their investigation as strong gun-control advocates, surprised and infuriated pro and antigun groups alike by concluding that there was "no compelling evidence that private weaponry is either an important cause of—or deterrent to—violent criminality."

The gun issue arouses intense, almost religious passions. Firearms clearly influence crime: If there were no guns, no crimes could be committed with them. Firearms are also inherently more lethal than other weapons. On the other hand, there are frequent reports of crimes being thwarted by armed self-defense. Personally, I'd prefer a less heavily armed nation, but the evidence shows that neither guns nor gun control contributes much to crime prevention.

HALF OF ALL HOUSEHOLDS FOR
TWENTY-FIVE YEARS

The best estimates of private firearms ownership place the number around 80 million in 1968, and 120 million in 1978, an increase of 40 million weapons (50 percent), which gun-control advocates decry as the "domestic arms race." There is, however, another side to the story. Every year since 1959, the Gallup Organization has asked a representative sample of Americans if they own any firearms. For twenty-five years, the response has been the same: About half of all households contain at least one. Fifty percent of all households were armed long before the FBI's dubious version of the crime rate began to accelerate in the mid-1960s. Today, with weapons sales at 4 million a year, about half of American households still are armed.

If 50 percent of the nation's homes have been armed for at least a generation, how can one account for the 40 million new firearms introduced since 1968? Almost all of the increase can be attributed to three factors: a 25 percent increase in the number of U.S. households since 1968 as the Baby Boom generation has set up housekeeping (half of *their* homes are armed); a 20 percent increase in the number of weapons per armed household; and substantial growth in the popularity of hunting and target-shooting. Increased recreational firearms demand alone accounts for nearly all the growth in shoulder weapons and one-third to one-half the growth in handguns. (Despite gun-control advocates' claims that "handguns have only one purpose—to kill people," sidearm hunting and target-shooting are quite popular.) Fear of crime has certainly motivated some people to purchase weapons, but surveys show that only about one weapon in four is purchased primarily for this reason.

Who owns all these guns? A cross section of the population, according to Wright and Rossi. Historically, gun owners have been "predominantly male, rural, Southern, Protestant, middle-class or affluent, and gun-sports oriented." But in recent years, the ranks of armed Americans have broadened to include many people once horrified by guns.

What are the nation's 60 million gun owners like? The research shows that their personality profiles are indistinct from those of the rest of the population. There is no evidence that gun owners are disproportionately unstable, violent, or maladapted. The idea that ordinary citizens are transformed into potential criminals when they acquire firearms seems far-fetched.

No credible observer would dispute the assertion that there are more guns, more gun owners, and more gun crimes in the United States than in any other nation. But what implications can be drawn from this? Wright and Rossi observe that two very different conclusions are possible, "either (a) that the need for strict gun control is self-evident, and would reduce violent crime, or (b) that the vast supply of arms already in private hands renders futile any government control efforts."

HANDGUNS AND CRIME: NO DIRECT RELATIONSHIP

Discussions of the gun issue invariably focus on handguns, the most easily concealed—and most criminally abused—firearms. Handguns comprise about one-third of the private arms supply, about 40 million weapons. If handgun ownership were directly associated with violent crime, one would expect that areas with highest per capita handgun ownership would have the highest rates of handgun crime. In fact, the *opposite* is the case. Handgun ownership is much more common in rural areas than in cities, yet urban residents are twice as likely to fall victim to violent crime.

Trends in the murder rates also cast doubt on handguns' purported role in violent crime. Since 1900, handgun ownership has not only increased every year, it has *accelerated* from 270,000 sales a year to more than two million today. Yet the violent crime rate (as measured by homicides) has fluctuated considerably. As discussed in chapter 3, the best predictor of violent crime is not the number of weapons available, but rather the number of people most likely to use them, young men in their prime crime years.

GUN LAWS: MINIMAL IMPACT ON CRIME

Handgun-control groups advocate purchase restrictions on and registration of sidearms, with greater government control over gun dealers. But even if handgun manufacture ceased immediately (politically impossible) and smuggling were completely prevented (also impossible), there would still be 40 million privately owned handguns in the United States. With reasonable maintenance, a sidearm can last more than a hundred years. Many Civil War pistols are still in fine working order today. The supply of weapons already available that *could* be used in crime is more than sufficient for the next several generations.

Progun organizations argue that *every* gun law is an unconstitutional violation of the Second Amendment, which, they say, gives Americans the right to bear arms. The Second Amendment notwithstanding, there are 20,000 local, state, and federal firearms laws on the books, and very few of them have ever been challenged, let alone struck down, as unconstitutional. The real question about gun laws turns not on their constitutionality, but on their effectiveness. Have they reduced the crime rate? The best evidence suggests that their impact has been minimal.

About 70 percent of the U.S. population lives in areas with laws regulating handgun purchases, and 60 percent is subject to prepurchase background checks. Yet the gun-crime problem is most serious in major cities, where gun laws are *strictest*. Gun-control advocates argue that this is the result of "patchwork" local and state laws, and they advocate federal legislation. But this reflects a serious misunderstanding of how most gun crimes occur. A tiny fraction—for example, gangland killings—may involve interstate transportation of weapons, but the typical street criminal almost always commits his crimes in his home community. The same is true of domestic violence. So-called comprehensive federal legislation would have no more impact on the vast majority of gun crimes than do local and state laws already on the books.

The federal Gun Control Act of 1968 (GCA) is our most sweeping handgun law. It banned the importation of foreign handguns (though not their parts). As a result, sales of foreign-assembled sidearms plummeted, but this decrease was more than offset by increased sales of domestically manufactured handguns and by sales of foreign guns assembled in the United States. Since the GCA, antigun activists have promoted a ban on the importation of foreign handgun parts, but such a law would have no effect on domestically manufactured sidearms, whose sales now total more than 2 million a year.

The Gun Control Act also banned mail-order handgun sales and tightened restrictions on gun dealers in hopes of restricting the flow of handguns to criminals. These provisions were based on the assumption that criminals purchase their guns from dealers. They don't. Most of the handguns used in crimes are stolen.

In 1976 Washington, D.C., adopted "the nation's toughest" handgun-control law. It limited sales to licensed dealers, and required registration and police review of purchase applications. A 1980 report by the U.S. Conference of Mayors credited the law with "a significant decrease in handgun crimes." But a more sophisticated analysis revealed that "most other jurisdictions (without tough handgun laws) showed decreases as well. Baltimore, perhaps the 'most appropriate' comparison city owing to its proximity, showed a more pronounced decline. Handgun homicides in Washington decreased 36 percent; in Baltimore, 46 percent."

Another type of gun-control law places restrictions not on weapons purchases per se, but on carrying them without a license. The best-known is Massachusetts' 1974 Bartley-Fox Amendment, which mandates a year in jail for unlicensed carrying, whether or not the weapon is used in a crime. Three before-and-after analyses of the law all reached somewhat different conclusions, but as a group, they show that Bartley-Fox had minimal impact on crime in the Bay State.

The final type of gun law focuses solely on the criminal abuse of firearms by increasing prison sentences for those convicted of gun crimes. "Use a gun, go to prison" laws enjoy broad support from people on both sides of the gun issue, but like all punishment meted out by the criminal justice system, they do little, if anything, to prevent gun crimes. In 1976, Detroit enacted a mandatory sentencing law for gun crimes that required two years in prison beyond other punishment. Violent crime decreased after its passage, but an evaluation concluded that the law "did not significantly alter the number or type of violent offenses." What reduced crime in Detroit was the racial integration of the police force and the Neighborhood Watch program, neither of which had anything to do with gun control or harsher punishments for criminals who use guns.

If it were possible to quickly and substantially reduce the number of handguns by, say, 50 percent, there would probably be fewer handgun crimes. But none of the laws designed to begin this process have had enough impact to justify the political firestorms they have caused. Our experience with Prohibition and the contemporary trafficking in illegal drugs shows that demand guarantees supply. Those who want guns will always be able to get them. Finally, studies show that even the toughest handgun controls do not reduce the rate of violent crimes. They simply shift the weapons mix slightly toward other weapons.

ARMED DETERRENCE: MINIMAL IMPACT ON CRIME

Advocates of gun ownership argue that private weaponry helps prevent political tyranny. An armed population *is* more difficult to subjugate than one without weapons. Progun people also insist that armed deterrence prevents a substantial proportion of crimes. However, the best evidence on this point suggests otherwise.

Victim studies show that armed deterrence prevents about 2 *percent* of robberies, and burglaries of occupied homes—about 25,000 robberies and burglaries in 1980—but is this significant? The National Rifle Association, with its strong "guns deter crime" position would answer with a resounding yes. But a 2 percent deterrence rate pales next to the 7-Eleven and Detroit programs that cut crime rates *in half* without firearms.

Armed deterrence also raises questions about injuries to innocent bystanders. Gun-control advocates often cite this statistic: "A gun in the home is five times more likely to harm a loved one than an intruder." This, however, is grossly misleading. It is based on one study of Cuyahoga County (Cleveland), Ohio, that compared the number of burglars shot in the act one year to *all gun injuries* to county residents, including suicides, hunting accidents, and injuries to policemen in the line of duty; *not* just gun injuries to bystanders when weapons were fired at criminals. Every year since 1953, firearms have accounted for about 2 percent of all accidental deaths, mostly hunting accidents. Gun owners should certainly exercise supreme caution (see "Basic Firearm Safety"), but the thirty-year stability of the accidental-gun-death rate in the context of accelerating handgun sales suggests that gun-control advocates have overstated the problem of injuries to innocent bystanders.

Should anyone purchase a firearm solely for protection against crime? Without a gun, under certain circumstances, you might experience a self-defense disadvantage, but your risk of causing a firearm accident would be zero. With a gun, your self-defense ability increases somewhat, but so does your risk of involvement in a gun accident. Either way, costs and benefits must be weighed. In the final analysis, gun ownership is a personal decision.

GUNS AND DOMESTIC VIOLENCE: THE CULMINATION, NOT THE CAUSE

At first glance, handgun control might appear to be an integral part of the "opportunity removal" focus of this book. Even if gun restrictions have minimal impact on street crime, gun-control advocates argue, the fewer weapons there are, the fewer the opportunities for lethal domestic violence. This might be true if, like street crime, domestic violence were impulsive and opportunistic. But it isn't. No doubt some family shootings arise from truly trivial circumstances, and in some cases the mere presence of a firearm—or any weapon—might catalyze its use. But the relative rarity of domestic weapons use, in the context of the truly staggering amount of violence and number of weapons in American homes, strongly suggests that most domestic killings are not "crimes of passion" committed "in the heat of the moment." Because family homicides are neither impulsive nor opportunistic, removal of the gun, the supposed instrument of opportunity, would have little effect.

There's a better explanation of why handguns are the weapon of choice in domestic homicide. After years of escalating violence, one party *decides* to kill the other, then chooses the most effective means to do so. Wright and Rossi write:

The idea that domestic shootings are "crimes of passion" by normally nonviolent people is difficult to square with the Police Foundation study of family-member killings in Kansas City. No fewer than 85 percent were preceded by one other violent incident serious enough for the police to be called. (Fifty percent were preceded by *five or more* such incidents.) It is not hard to imagine that many of these homicides involved [a battered woman telling her husband], "If you do that again, I'm going to kill you." He does, then she does.

The problem is not simply *gun* violence, as ghastly and lethal as it often is; the real problem is *all* violence. After all, 50 percent of murders *do not* involve handguns. Aren't they just as tragic as those that do?

Given an understanding of battering relationships, it's clear that restrictions on handgun ownership would have little effect on most domestic violence, more than 95 percent of which does not involve weapons. With regard to family murder, handgun restrictions would probably have two effects: a smaller proportion of gun homicides offset by increases in knife, shoulder weapon, and blunt-instrument killings; and a greater proportion of women victims, since wives would be less able to defend against battering spouses with weapons other than handguns, which depend more on physical strength. (For this reason, some counselors of battered women oppose handgun controls as discriminatory against women, the elderly, and the disabled.)

The most constructive approaches to domestic violence have nothing to do with restricting access to handguns. They involve better public understanding of battering relationships, earlier intervention by police and community agencies, and improved support resources for battered women and battering men.

THE REAL WEAPONS PROBLEM: GUN THEFT

The real problem with guns has nothing to do with their private possession per se, but rather with their criminal abuse. How do street criminals *actually obtain* their weapons? Police say that 25 to 50 percent of crime guns are stolen. That estimate turns out to be quite conservative.

About 275,000 guns are stolen every year. Wright and Rossi asked two thousand prison inmates convicted of gun crimes how they obtained their weapons. Almost all said they'd either stolen them or bought stolen weapons from other criminals. The study also reconfirmed the opportunistic nature of street crime: "Practically none of the criminals said they'd consciously gone out looking to steal firearms," Wright said. "If they found them, they took them. And with half of all homes armed, the chances of a burglar finding a gun are pretty good."

The fundamental premise of this book is that the best way to reduce the crime rate is for each of us to incorporate a crime-prevention program into our life. For gun owners, this certainly includes proper gun security. The burglar who steals a firearm probably lives within a mile or two of the burglarized home. If that weapon is used in a crime, chances are the crime will occur in the same general vicinity. Gun security, therefore, is crucial to gun owners' own neighborhood security.

Gun owners not only have a moral responsibility to secure their weapons, they may also be held liable if a crime gun can be traced to them. In 1982 a U.S. District Court ordered the National Rifle Association to pay $2 million in damages to the family of a man killed in a holdup with a handgun stolen during a burglary of NRA headquarters.

There are several ways to secure firearms:

• *Store weapons in locked, high-security cabinets.* Gun safes are available through gun shops and gun magazines. Many can be bolted to walls or floors, and feature reinforced steel walls and top-rated Medeco locks. Gun safes cost $250 to $500, a reasonable investment considering the value of many weapons—and the risk to you and your neighbors if any of your weapons are stolen.

• *Never leave weapons accessible.* If you truly believe that you're safer sleeping with a loaded gun by your bed, remove the weapon from secure storage and load it before you retire, then unload and resecure it each morning. This involves little more effort than brushing your teeth. If you prefer to keep a gun handy, and not locked away, construct a secure hiding place (see chapter 5), then equip every weapon with a trigger lock, so it cannot be fired by anyone, particularly a child who might happen to find it.

• *Rigorous target-hardening and community organizing.* Weapons per se won't keep anyone out of your home or neighborhood. The suggestions in chapters 4 through 7 will.

Most of the nation's 120 million private firearms do not fall into criminal hands. Still, every year 275,000 do, and each year about four hundred children are killed playing with improperly secured weapons. Can anything be done to encourage better gun security among the small but highly significant proportion of gun owners who do not take adequate precautions? One possibility might be to hold the owner liable as an accessory to any crime committed with a gun traced to him (or her), as in the NRA case. But given the impossibility of registering all the weapons in private hands, tracing the ownership of more than a tiny fraction of crime guns seems utopian, especially since many gun owners would remove identifying markings to prevent such liability. Another approach might be to penalize gun owners who reported their weapons stolen. But this would certainly be challenged as a violation of the Fifth Amendment, which protects against self-incrimination.

There is, however, one simple approach that would in no way threaten the right to bear arms, yet at the same time would encourage gun owners who do not already do so to store their weapons more securely. As discussed in chapter 5, the government could prohibit the insurance industry from providing gun owners with weapons-theft coverage unless their homes were adequately target-hardened and/or unless the firearms were stolen by breaking into a gun safe. The typical homeowner's policy provides $1,000–$2,000 coverage for firearms without regard to target-hardening or gun security. If this coverage were contingent on a simple document signed by a local crime-prevention officer that the owner had a gun safe capable of housing all his weapons and had implemented the recommendations of a home security survey, it would pose no threat whatsoever to private weapons ownership, nor would it deny insurance coverage to gun owners whose weapons might be quite valuable. It *would*, however, encourage better gun (and home) security. Of course, there is no guarantee that security requirements for firearms coverage would, in fact, reduce weapons thefts. This plan requires only that appropriate target-hardening and gun-security equipment be installed, not that it actually be *used*. Nonetheless, this modest proposal would be a step in the right direction. It would probably reduce criminal access to firearms, and it focuses on the real weapons problem, not gun ownership but gun theft.

BASIC FIREARM SAFETY

Many of those who purchase firearms for self-protection already own other sporting weapons and are presumably trained in their use. Gun owners have a responsibility to become intimately familiar with their weapons and to practice regularly to decrease the risk of accidents. Practice is particularly important for first-time gun buyers. Every first-time handgun owner should take a course in handgun safety; in fact, the *entire family* should. Children are naturally curious about firearms. Gun training satisfies their curiosity, while teaching the proper respect for firearms that helps prevent accidents.

If you decide to incorporate a firearm into your personal crime-prevention program, the first decision is to choose between a shoulder weapon and a handgun. Among shoulder weapons, most authorities would recommend a shotgun. Shotguns cover a wider field than rifles, thus largely eliminating the need for precise aiming, often a problem at night, in the dark, when one is anxious about an intruder in the house. Shotgun shell pellet size can also be controlled to minimize injury risk to bystanders. Most shotgun pellets do not penetrate walls and doors as easily as rifle bullets. The major disadvantages of shotguns are their bulk and recoil, which may make them unwieldy for some people.

Among handguns, most authorities would recommend a .38 caliber double-action revolver. "Double-action" means that one squeeze on the trigger both cocks the hammer and releases it. Most police discourage automatic pistols for home defense because of the significant risk of leaving a shell in the firing chamber by accident.

I have never owned any firearms, but to do research for this book, I enrolled in a handgun safety class. The four-hour, $45 course was taught by off-duty officers of the San Francisco Police Department. About twelve of my fifteen classmates were men, and nine had enrolled to meet security-guard job requirements. (This surprised me. I thought there would be more prospective home defenders.)

The officers lectured on the safe operation of the various types of handguns, then positioned us on the firing range. Using the school's .38 caliber double-action revolvers, we shot at paper targets printed with human silhouettes. Once we felt comfortable firing and reloading, the range officer dimmed the lights until we were shooting in near darkness, to simulate the firing conditions of being awakened at night by an intruder. Then we learned to clean and oil the weapons.

One aspect of the course came as a revelation to me. Behind the lectern stood a thick, solid-core exterior door, the kind recommended in the target-hardening section of chapter 5. The door had a dozen holes through it, each labeled with a different type of handgun bullet fired from a distance of twenty feet. (Studies show that police rarely fire their revolvers at people more than seven yards away.) *Every bullet went right through the door, even the smallest .22.* Any bullet can travel through several walls. Weapons fired at criminals can injure children in the next room or neighbors two houses down the street.

In many states, it's a felony to shoot a robber or burglar unless the shooter can persuade the district attorney (or a jury) that his or her life was in grave and imminent danger—the theory being that no one has a right to take a life in defense of property, only in defense of life. As a result, the officers urged our class to adopt "staggered loading": birdshot (shotgun-type ammunition) for the first three rounds, then bullets thereafter. When fired, birdshot disperses into a hail of shrapnel that usually stops an assailant without killing him. Birdshot does not penetrate most walls and doors, thus reducing the risk of injury to bystanders. If, after three rounds of birdshot, the assailant kept approaching (or brandished a weapon), a reasonable person could presume a threat to life, and by the fourth round, a bullet would have entered the firing chamber.

The text booklet, "Set Your Sights on Handgun Basics," dealt mostly with sidearm hunting and target-shooting. But it didn't mince words about armed self-defense: "Without a doubt personal protection is the most controversial use of handguns. A person who faces a possibly life-threatening situation must carefully consider the decision to use a handgun. Police receive many hours of training before they can deal with assailants. You must expect to do the same. In most situations, there is no need to use a firearm for self-defense." From "Set Your Sights," here are the Ten Commandments of Gun Safety:

1. Always treat every gun as if it is loaded.
2. Always keep the barrel pointed in a safe direction—down and away from all living things.
3. Never place a finger on the trigger until ready to fire at a proper target.
4. Keep the safety on and/or the action (cylinder or other firing system) open unless firing.
5. Know your target and backstop. Never shoot at anything you cannot see clearly.
6. Know your weapon and its ammunition.
7. Always transport weapons unloaded, preferably with the action open.
8. Always keep the barrel and action clean.
9. Never shoot at water or flat surfaces from which bullets might ricochet.
10. Guns and alcohol (and other drugs) don't mix. Never use any drugs around firearms.

THE BEST WAY TO REDUCE GUN CRIMES

The "guns vs. gun control" debate will undoubtedly rage as long as gun crimes are committed. But like the polarization between liberals and conservatives, it is largely beside the point. At best, both armed deterrence and gun control reduce violent crime by a few percentage points. Programs based on secondary crime prevention, however, quickly reduce it 30 to 60 percent without arming or disarming anyone.

One key to crime prevention is neighborhood cohesion. The tragedy of the gun debate is that it has alienated neighbors from one another. It has led each side in the gun controversy to stereotype the other. Gun owners sometimes dismiss gun-control advocates as "unpatriotic fools with no respect for the Constitution." Gun-control advocates sometimes view gun owners as "bloodthirsty psychopaths." Both of these stereotypes are absurd. Half the nation's households have been armed for at least twenty-five years, and no matter what any individual decides about firearms ownership, it's quite clear that gun owners and nonowners alike are average, normal people from all walks of life.

It's time we stopped fighting about the gun issue and concentrated on fighting crime. Neither armed deterrence nor gun control reduce the crime rate anywhere near as effectively as the crime-prevention alternatives discussed throughout this book. We *can* reduce the crime rate quickly and substantially, but only if we work together.

Resources:

Under the Gun
by James D. Wright, Peter H. Rossi, and Kathleen
Daly, with Eleanor Weber-Burdin
1983, 360 pages, $24.95
Aldine Publishing Company
200 Saw Mill River Rd.
Hawthorne, NY 10532

The book on the gun issue. Don't take my word for the fact that guns neither cause nor prevent a significant amount of crime. Examine the research and decide for yourself.

"Set Your Sights on Handgun Basics"
1980, 47 pages, inquire about price from
Outdoor Empire Publishing, Inc.
P. O. Box C–19000
Seattle, WA 98109
(206) 624–3845

A good introduction to handgun operation and safety.

CONCLUSION

Much Safer Starting Today

FROM "THEM" TO "US"

Most discussions of crime frame the problem in terms of "us *vs.* them." It's those bad people preying on us good people, with the evil ones much different from the rest of us: "drug addicts," "sociopaths," "the dregs of society." Some criminals fit these descriptions, but such stereotypes seriously limit our understanding of the crime problem—and how best to deal with it. The problem lies not just with "them," but more than we'd care to admit, with *all of us*.

Crime is, and always has been, a fairly normal, if unwelcome, part of growing up—not just for ghetto youth, those most likely to be turned into "examples" by the courts, but for everyone. In a classic study, a large representative sample of adults was asked if they'd ever committed any of forty-nine crimes since age sixteen. Fully 91 *percent* admitted having committed at least one. The average man admitted to eighteen offenses, the average woman, eleven. Here are their admission rates:

Offense	*% Men*	*% Women*
Theft	89	83
Disorderly conduct	85	76

220

Offense	% Men	% Women
Vandalism	84	82
Income tax evasion	57	40
Assault	49	5
Fraud	46	34
Concealed weapons	35	3
Perjury	23	17
Burglary	17	4
Grand larceny	13	11
Robbery	11	1

What do these statistics demonstrate? The lawlessness of the generation that came of age during the turbulent Vietnam era? Not quite. The figures would be disturbing no matter when they were compiled, but what makes this survey truly astonishing is that it was published in *1947*. The subjects committed their crimes during the relatively tranquil 1930s and 1940s, a generation before "law and order" became a national issue.

Since this study, the role of crime in American adolescence has remained about the same. For a majority of Americans (especially men), crime has always been a dubious rite of passage into adulthood. This in no way excuses it, or compels us to resign ourselves to victimization. But it illustrates that the problem involves not only "those ghetto youth," "those drug addicts," or "those incorrigibles." It involves everyone. There are, of course, degrees of wrongdoing. But the point is that anyone can succumb to impulse and opportunity. Most of us have.

FIFTY PERCENT IN FIVE YEARS

The myth that the responsibility for crime lies outside ourselves with "them," has an equally damaging corollary, that the responsibility for preventing crime also lies beyond us, with the government, the criminal justice system, the schools, and social agencies. Their work is certainly important, but they cannot take primary responsibility for crime control. That responsibility belongs to each one of us.

There is no mystery to crime prevention. Anyone can practice street awareness, target-hardening, and neighborhood organizing. These skills are easy to learn and fulfilling to share. They empower us to exercise greater control over our lives.

Individual and neighborhood crime prevention has an impressive record. Crime-rate reductions of more than 50 percent are common. If, as a nation, we committed ourselves to the effort, we could cut the crime rate in half in five years.

The tools are at our disposal. The task lies before us. We can all become much safer. Let's get to work. *Now.*

Bibliography

BOOKS

Adams, Caren, and Jennifer Fay. *No More Secrets: Protecting Your Child from Sexual Assault.* San Luis Obispo, Calif.: Impact Publishing, 1981.

Bach, George R., and Peter Wyden. *The Intimate Enemy.* New York: Avon, 1968.

Bard, Morton, and Dawn Sangrey. *The Crime Victim's Book.* New York: Basic Books, 1979.

Bennett, Georgette. *A Safe Place to Live.* New York: Insurance Information Institute, 1982.

Browning, Frank, and John Gerassi. *The American Way of Crime.* New York: Putnam, 1980.

Brownmiller, Susan. *Against Our Will: Men, Women, and Rape.* New York: Bantam, 1976.

Clark, Ramsey. *Crime in America.* New York: Pocket Books, 1971.

Consumer Reports. 1982 Buying Guide. Mount Vernon, N.Y.: Consumers Union, 1982.

Cronin, Thomas E., Tania Z. Cronin, and Michael E. Milakovich. *U.S. v. Crime in the Streets.* Bloomington, Ind.: Indiana University Press, 1981.

Dobson, Terry, with Judith Shepherd-Chow. *Safe and Alive: How to Protect Yourself, Your Family, and Your Property Against Violence.* Los Angeles: Tarcher, 1981.

Eysenck, H. J., and D. K. B. Nias. *Sex, Violence, and the Media.* New York: Harper Colophon, 1978.

Fein, Judith. *Are You a Target?* Belmont, Calif.: Wadsworth, 1981.

Frankel, William, ed. *Home Security.* Alexandria, Va.: Time-Life Books, 1979.

Goldstein, Jeffry H. *Aggression and Crimes of Violence.* New York: Oxford University Press, 1975.

Gottman, John, et al. *A Couple's Guide to Communication.* Champaign, Ill.: Research Press, 1976.

Griffith, Liddon R. *Mugging: You Can Protect Yourself.* Englewood Cliffs, N.J.: Prentice-Hall, 1978.

Groth, A. Nicholas, with H. Jean Birnbaum. *Men Who Rape: The Psychology of the Offender.* New York: Plenum Press, 1980.

Guarino, Vincent J. *Everyman's Guide to Better Home Security.* Boulder, Colo.: Paladin Press, 1981.

Hampden-Turner, Charles. *Sane Asylum: Inside the Delancey Street Foundation.* San Francisco: San Francisco Book Company, 1976.

Helfer, Ray E., and C. Henry Kempe, eds. *The Battered Child.* 2d ed. Chicago: University of Chicago Press, 1974.

Hjersman, Peter. *The Stash Book: How to Hide Your Valuables.* Berkeley, Calif.: And/Or Press, 1978.

Jackson, Bruce. *A Thief's Primer.* New York: Macmillan, 1969.

Johnson, Ray. *Too Dangerous to Be at Large.* New York: Quadrangle, 1975.

Justice, Blair, and Rita Blair. *The Abusing Family.* New York: Human Sciences Press, 1976.

Keogh, James E., and John Koster. *Burglarproof: A Complete Guide to Home Security.* New York: McGraw-Hill, 1977.

Leonard, George. *The Silent Pulse.* New York: Bantam, 1981.

LeShan, Edna. *The Roots of Crime.* New York: Four Winds Press, 1981.

Mager, N. H., and S. K. Mager. *Protect Yourself: The Complete Guide to Safeguarding Your Life and Home.* New York: Dell, 1978.

Martin, Del. *Battered Wives.* New York: Pocket Books, 1977.

Menninger, Karl. *The Crime of Punishment.* New York: Penguin, 1968.

McDonald, Hugh C. *Survival.* New York: Ballantine, 1982.

Miller Curt, *Total Home Protection.* Farmington, Mich.: Structures Publishing, 1976.

Mitford, Jessica. *Kind and Unusual Punishment: The Prison Business.* New York: Vintage, 1974.

Murphy, Patrick, and Thomas Plate. *Commissioner: A View from the Top of American Law Enforcement.* New York: Simon & Schuster, 1977.

Newman, Oscar. *Defensible Space: Crime Prevention Through Urban Design.* New York: Collier/Macmillan, 1973.

NiCarthy, Ginny. *Getting Free: A Handbook for Women in Abusive Relationships.* Seattle: Seal Press, 1982.

Ratledge, Marcus Wayne. *Don't Become the Victim.* Boulder, Colo.: Paladin Press, 1981.

Rhodes, Robert P. *The Insoluble Problems of Crime.* New York: Wiley, 1977.

Shields, Pete. *Guns Don't Die—People Do.* New York: Priam/Arbor House, 1981.

Silberman, Charles E. *Criminal Violence, Criminal Justice.* New York: Vintage, 1978.

Sliwa, Curtis and Murray Schwartz. *Streetsmart: The Guardian Angel Guide to Safe Living.* Reading, Mass.: Addison-Wesley, 1982.

Sloane, Eugene A. *The Complete Book of Locks, Keys, Burglar and Smoke Alarms, and Other Security Devices.* New York: William Morrow, 1977.

Sonkin, Daniel Jay, and Michael Durphy. *Learning to Live Without Violence: A Handbook for Men.* San Francisco: Volcano Press, 1982.

Speriglio, Milo, and S. Thomas Eubanks. *How to Protect Your Life and Property.* Sherman Oaks, Calif.: Seville Publishing, 1982.

Storaska, Frederic. *How to Say No to a Rapist—and Survive.* New York: Random House, 1975.

Straus, Murray A., Richard J. Gelles, and Suzanne K. Steinmetz. *Behind Closed Doors: Violence in the American Family.* Garden City, N.Y.: Anchor/Doubleday, 1981.

Vetter, Harold J., and Ira J. Silverman. *The Nature of Crime.* Philadephia: W. B. Saunders, 1978.

Walker, Lenore. *The Battered Woman.* New York: Harper Colophon, 1979.

Wilson, James Q. *Thinking About Crime.* New York: Vintage. 1977.

Wright, James D., Peter H. Rossi, and Kathleen Daly, with Eleanor Weber Burdin. *Under the Gun: Weapons, Crime and Violence in America.* Hawthorne, N.Y.: Aldine Publishing, 1983.

REPORTS AND ARTICLES

Auletta, Kenneth. "The Underclass," *The New Yorker,* Nov. 16, 1981.

Beedle, Steve. "Evaluation of the Home Security Program, Supplemental Report," Portland Police Crime Prevention Detail, Portland, Ore., May 1981.

Beedle, Steve, and Jan Stangier. "Evaluation of the Home Security Program," Portland Police Crime Prevention Detail, Portland, Ore., Oct. 1980.

Biderman, A. "Social Change Indicators and Goals," in *Social Indicators,* R. A. Bauer, ed., MIT Press, Cambridge, Mass., 1966.

Blumstein, A. "Crime, Punishment, and Demographics," *American Demographics,* Oct. 1980, p. 33.

Brenner, Harvey, "Mortality and the National Economy," *The Lancet,* Sept. 15, 1979.

California Commission on Crime Control and Violence Prevention. "An Ounce of Prevention: Toward an Understanding of the Causes of Violence," Office of Assemblyman John Vasconcellos, Sacramento, Calif., 1982.

Campaign for Economic Democracy. "The Crisis of Crime: A Call for Action," Santa Monica, Calif., May 1981.

Cedar Rapids Police Dept. "Evaluation of Burglar Alarm System," LEAA, U.S. Dept. of Justice, Dec. 1971.

Chamber of Commerce of the U.S. "Handbook on White Collar Crime," Washington, D.C., 1972.

Chelimsky, Eleanor, et al. "Security and the Small Business Retailer," prepared by The Mitre Corporation, McLean, Va., for the U.S. Department of Justice, June 1978.

Chira, S., "TV Fantasy vs. Reality: Kids Know the Difference," *New York Times*, Dec. 3, 1982.

Community United Against Violence, "CUAV Assault Report Survey and Analysis," CUAV, San Francisco, Calif., 1980.

Emerge—Men's Counseling Service on Domestic Violence. "Organizing and Implementing Services for Men Who Batter," Emerge, Boston, Mass., 1981.

Federal Bureau of Investigation. "Crime in the United States, 1980," U.S. Department of Justice, Washington, D.C., Sept. 1981.

Garofalo, James, and Kevin J. Connelly. "Dispute Resolution Centers," reprinted from *Criminal Justice Abstracts*, National Council on Crime and Delinquency, Hackensack, N.J., Sept. 1980.

Gelber, Seymour. "Treating Juvenile Crime," Op/Ed p., *New York Times*, Dec. 12, 1981.

Gordon, Diana, R. "Doing Violence to the Crime Problem: A Response to the Attorney General's Task Force," National Council on Crime and Delinquency, Hackensack, N.J., Sept. 1981.

Grayson, B., and M. Stein, "Attracting Assault: Victims' Nonverbal Cues," *Journal of Communication*, Winter 1981, p. 74.

Highway Data Loss Institute. "Insurance Losses and Theft Coverage: Passenger Cars, Vans, Pickups, and Utility Vehicles," HDLI, Washington, D.C., May 1982.

Institute for the Community as Extended Family. "Parents United: Professional Introductory Packet," San Jose, Calif.

Kempe, C. Henry. "The Battered Child Syndrome," *Journal of the American Medical Association*, July 1962, pp, 105–12.

Kent, Cordelia A. "Child Sexual Abuse Prevention Project: An Education Program for Children," Office of the Hennepin County Attorney, Minneapolis, Minn., 1979.

Mallowe, M. "The Burglar," *Philadelphia Magazine*, May 1981, p. 130.

Martinson, Robert, et al. "Rehabilitation, Recidivism, and Research," National Council on Crime and Delinquency, Hackensack, N.J., 1976.

National Advisory Committee on Criminal Justice Standards and Goals. "Private Security: Report of the Task Force on Private Security," U.S. Department of Justice, Washington, D.C., Dec. 1976.

National Coalition on Television Violence. "TV Violence All-Time High," In NCTV News, Decatur, Ill., March-May 1982.

National Institute of Justice. "The Link Between Crime and the Built Environment," U.S. Department of Justice, Washington, D.C., Dec. 1980.

National Institute of Law Enforcement and Criminal Justice."Commercial Security Test Design," U.S. Department of Justice, Washington, D.C., May 1979.

———. "Crime Prevention Handbook for Senior Citizens," U.S. Department of Justice, Washington, D.C., 1977.

National Institute of Mental Health. "Television and Behavior: Ten Years of Scientific Progress and Implications for the '80s," U.S. Department of Health and Human Services, Washington, D.C., 1982.

Newton, Anne M. "Prevention of Crime and Delinquency," reprinted from *Criminal Justice Abstracts*, National Council on Crime and Delinquency, Hackensack, N.J., June 1978.

Office of Community Crime Prevention. "We Can Prevent Crime," Law Enforcement Assistance Administration, U.S. Department of Justice, Washington, D.C., 1979.

Phelan, Patricia, and Bruce Joyce. "The Child Sexual Abuse Treatment Program Model: Clients, Treatment, and Family Growth," The Scripps Center, Palo Alto, Calif., Jan. 1980.

Pope, Carl E. "Crime-Specific Analysis: An Empirical Examination of Burglary Offender Characteristics," National Criminal Justice Information and Statistics Service, U.S. Department of Justice, Washington, D.C., 1977.

Queens Bench Foundation. "Rape: Prevention and Resistance," San Francisco, Calif., 1976.

Schnelle, J. F. "Evaluation of Two Patrolling Strategies," *Journal of Applied Behavior Analysis*, 8 (4), 1975.

Selkin, J. "Protecting Personal Space: Victim and Resistor Reactions in Rape," *Journal of Communication*, 6:1978.

Shonholtz, Raymond. "A Criminal Justice System That Isn't Working and Its Impact on the Community," The Community Boards Program, San Francisco, Calif.

Stangier, Jan, and Steve Beedle. "Institutionalization: A Survey of Community Attitudes toward Crime Prevention," Portland Police Crime Prevention Detail, Portland, Ore., March 1981.

———. "Evaluation of the Commercial Security Survey Program," Portland Police Crime Prevention Detail, Portland, Ore., June 1981.

U.S. Bureau of the Census. "Criminal Victimization in the United States, 1979," prepared for the Bureau of Justice Statistics, U.S. Department of Justice, Washington, D.C., Sept. 1981.

Wallerstein, J. S., and J. Wyle. "Our Law-Abiding Lawbreakers," *Probation*, 25:107–12, 1947.

Western Behavior Sciences Institute. "Summary of the Final Report: Robbery Deterrence, An Applied Behavioral Science Demonstration." La Jolla, Calif., Sept. 29, 1975.

Wilson, James Q., and Barbara Boland. "The Effect of Police on Crime," Law Enforcement Assistance Administration, U.S. Department of Justice, Washington, D.C., Nov. 1979.

Wilson, James Q., and George Kelling. "Broken Windows: The Police and Neighborhood Safety," *The Atlantic Monthly*, March 1982.

Wise, James. "A Gentle Deterrent of Vandalism," *Psychology Today*, Sept. 1982, pp. 31–38.

Wright, James D., and Peter Rossi, with Kathleen Daly and Eleanor Weber-Burdin. "Weapons, Crime and Violence in America," National Institute of Justice, U.S. Department of Justice, Washington, D.C., Nov. 1981.

Index

229

About the Author

Michael Castleman, one of the nation's foremost self-help writers, is the Managing Editor of *Medical Self-Care Magazine* (Inverness, California), and the author of *Sexual Solutions: An Informative Guide* (Touchstone/Simon & Schuster, 1983). His work has appeared in the *New York Times* and many other newspapers and magazines. His crime-prevention experience includes community organizing in Michigan and San Francisco, martial arts training, consultation with community crime-prevention groups around the country, and participation in the Community Boards Program, a neighborhood conflict-resolution organization in San Francisco, where he lives with his wife.

TO CONTACT THE AUTHOR

Write to: Michael Castleman, 55 Sutter St., Suite 645, San Francisco, CA 94104. Only selected correspondence can be answered.